THE PETROLEUM
EXPERIENCE OF
ABU DHABI

THE PETROLEUM EXPERIENCE OF ABU DHABI

WITHDRAWN

Atef Suleiman

THE EMIRATES CENTER FOR STRATEGIC
STUDIES AND RESEARCH

THE EMIRATES CENTER FOR STRATEGIC STUDIES AND RESEARCH

The Emirates Center for Strategic Studies and Research (ECSSR) is an independent research institution dedicated to the promotion of professional studies and educational excellence in the UAE, the Gulf and the Arab world. Since its establishment in Abu Dhabi in 1994, the ECSSR has served as a focal point for scholarship on political, economic and social matters. Indeed, the ECSSR is at the forefront of analysis and commentary on Arab affairs.

The Center seeks to provide a forum for the scholarly exchange of ideas by hosting conferences and symposia, organizing workshops, sponsoring a lecture series and publishing original and translated books and research papers. The ECSSR also has an active fellowship and grant program for the writing of scholarly books and for the translation into Arabic of work relevant to the Center's mission. Moreover, the ECSSR has a large library including rare and specialized holdings, and a state-of-the-art technology center, which has developed an award-winning website that is a unique and comprehensive source of information on the Gulf.

Through these and other activities, the ECSSR aspires to engage in mutually beneficial professional endeavors with comparable institutions worldwide, and to contribute to the general educational and academic development of the UAE.

The views expressed in this book do not necessarily reflect those of the ECSSR.

First published in 2007 by
The Emirates Center for Strategic Studies and Research
PO Box 4567, Abu Dhabi, United Arab Emirates

E-mail: pubdis@ecssr.ae
Website: http://www.ecssr.ae

Cover images courtesy of Abu Dhabi Gas Liquefaction Company (ADGAS) and the Center for Documentation and Research.

ISBN: 978-9948-00-911-5

Contents

FIGURES AND TABLES

TABLES

.

ABBREVIATIONS AND ACRONYMS

ADCCAC	Abu Dhabi Commercial Conciliation and Arbitration Center
ADDCAP	Abu Dhabi Drilling Chemicals and Projects Limited
ADCO	Abu Dhabi Company for Onshore Oil Operations
ADGAS	Abu Dhabi Gas Liquefaction Company
ADIA	Abu Dhabi Investment Authority
ADMA	Abu Dhabi Marine Areas Ltd.
ADMA-OPCO	Abu Dhabi Marine Operating Company
ADNATCO	Abu Dhabi National Tankers Company
ADNOC	Abu Dhabi National Oil Company
ADOCO	Abu Dhabi Oil Co. (Japan) Ltd.
ADPC	Abu Dhabi Petroleum Company Ltd.
ADPPOC	Abu Dhabi Petroleum Ports Operating Company (see IRSHAD)
ADWEA	Abu Dhabi Water and Electricity Authority
AIOC	Anglo-Iranian Oil Company
AMINOIL	American Independent Oil Company
API	American Petroleum Institute
APOC	Anglo-Persian Oil Company (later re-named AIOC)
Aramco	Arabian American Oil Company
ARE	Arab Republic of Egypt
BAPCO	Bahrain Petroleum Company
Borouge	Abu Dhabi Polymers Company Limited
BP	British Petroleum
bpd	barrels per day
Btu	British thermal units
CCC	Consolidated Construction Company

CFP	Compagnie Francaise des Petroles
cfpd	cubic feet per day
CFR	cost and freight
CIF	cost, insurance and freight
COA	contract of affreightment
CVP	Corporación Venezolana de Petroleo (Venezuela)
DEL	Dolphin Energy Ltd.
EGPC	Egyptian Petroleum Corporation
ENI	Ente Nazionale Idrocarburi
FERTIL	Ruwais Fertilizer Industries
FOB	free on board
GASCO	Abu Dhabi Gas Industries Limited
GCC	Gulf Cooperation Council
GSPA	gas supply and payment agreement
HSE	health, safety and environment
HSEMS	Health, Safety and Environment Management System
ICC	International Chamber of Commerce
ICJ	International Court of Justice
ICSID	International Centre for the Settlement of Investment Disputes
IPC	Iraq Petroleum Company
IPIC	International Petroleum Investment Company
IRSHAD	Abu Dhabi Petroleum Ports Operating Company (formerly ADPPOC)
JMC	Joint Management Committee
JOC	Joint Operating Company
JODCO	Japan Oil Development Company
kbpd	thousand barrels per day
KNPC	Kuwait National Petroleum Company

KOC	Kuwait Oil Company
LGSC	Liquefied Gas Shipping Company Limited
LIAMCO	Libyan American Oil Company
LNG	liquefied natural gas
LPG	liquefied petroleum gas
mbpd	million barrels per day
NDC	National Drilling Company
NGL	natural gas liquid
NIOC	National Iranian Oil Company
NMS	National Marine Services
NPCC	National Petroleum Construction Company
OAPEC	Organization of Arab Petroleum Exporting Countries
OPCO	operating company
OPEC	Organization of the Petroleum Exporting Countries
PD(TC)	Petroleum Development (Trucial Coast) Ltd.
PCIJ	Permanent Court of International Justice
PETROMIN	General Petroleum and Mineral Organization
PSA	production-sharing agreement
QPC	Qatar Petroleum Company
ro-ro	roll-on / roll-off
SAMAREC	Saudi Arabian Marketing and Refining Company
SPC	Supreme Petroleum Council
TEPCO	Tokyo Electric Power Company Inc.
UDECO	Umm Al-Dalkh Development Company
UNCITRAL	UN Commission on International Trade Law
UOG	UAE Offset Group
VLCCs	very large crude carriers
ZADCO	Zakum Development Company

FOREWORD

The United Arab Emirates (UAE) is one of the world's major oil-producing countries. A member of the Organization of the Petroleum Exporting Countries (OPEC) and of the Organization of Arab Petroleum Exporting Countries (OAPEC), the UAE has estimated recoverable oil reserves of around 97 billion barrels, of which the emirate of Abu Dhabi alone accounts for around 92 billion barrels.

In the early years of hydrocarbon exploration and production, Abu Dhabi's oil industry was dominated by major international oil companies operating under concession agreements with the emirate, as was the case elsewhere in the Middle East region. The control exercised by these super companies – the 'Majors,' as they were known – was total, leaving host governments with little or no say in decisions relating to the exploitation of their own natural resources.

A number of important events that took place between 1950 and 1970 were to bring about a radical change in the old concession system. The establishment of OPEC in 1960 and the passing of United Nations General Assembly Resolution No. 2158 of 1966 calling for governments to exercise sovereignty over their natural resources, culminated in a trend of 'participation' by governments in activities relating to their oil and gas industries.

National Oil Companies (NOCs) established by the oil-producing states formalized this trend, providing governments with greater control over oil and gas production in their territories. Some states achieved complete nationalization of their hydrocarbon reserves, and gradually the national governments of the Middle East reclaimed state control over their respective oil and gas industries.

The petroleum experience of Abu Dhabi has been varied and extensive. Over the years, the structure of the industry has slowly developed, from the original concession arrangements through to the establishment of the Abu Dhabi National Oil Company (ADNOC) and its subsidiaries. During this transformation of the industry in Abu Dhabi, the legal framework governing the development of petroleum resources in the emirate has evolved, as has the tax system applicable to operating companies, the means of dispute resolution, and the overall organizational structure of the industry.

This study of the petroleum experience of Abu Dhabi explores this evolution and analyzes the growth of an industry which has shaped the development of today's UAE federation.

A word of thanks is due to ECSSR editor Francis Field for coordinating the publication of this book.

Jamal S. Al-Suwaidi, Ph.D.
Director General
ECSSR

INTRODUCTION

This book provides a study of the petroleum experience of the emirate of Abu Dhabi, part of the United Arab Emirates (UAE). It aims to shed light on certain aspects of this experience, including the underlying principles of Abu Dhabi's oil policy and the different achievements of the emirate's oil industry. The study of the legal aspects of the experience and the legal framework for the development of petroleum resources in the emirate will constitute an important part of the work.

The emirate of Abu Dhabi is one of seven emirates that constitute the United Arab Emirates (UAE)—Abu Dhabi, Dubai, Sharjah, Ras Al Khaimah, Ajman, Fujairah and Umm Al Qawain. The UAE is a large oil producer in a major producing area – the Arabian Gulf – and a member of both the Organization of the Petroleum Exporting Countries (OPEC) and the Organization of Arab Petroleum Exporting Countries (OAPEC). Abu Dhabi has been a member of OAPEC since 1970, and joined OPEC in 1967—membership of OPEC was taken over by the UAE federation in 1974.

The UAE possess huge reserves of oil and gas and enjoys a comfortable production capacity. Oil, in effect, is the corner-stone of the UAE economy. Oil was first discovered in Abu Dhabi in 1958 and production began in 1962 from offshore areas and then in 1963 from onshore fields. The oil sector developed very quickly and Abu Dhabi soon became a major world oil exporter. In Dubai, oil in commercial qualities was discovered in 1966 and the first cargo was shipped in 1969. Oil was subsequently discovered in Sharjah in 1972 and exports commenced in 1974. Ras Al Khaimah was the fourth emirate to discover and exploit oil in 1983.

Of the seven emirates comprising the UAE, Abu Dhabi possesses the largest oil and gas reserves and is the principal producer. While the proven crude oil reserves of the UAE are presently estimated at around 97 billion barrels, Abu Dhabi alone accounts for 92.2 billion barrels of crude oil reserves. Despite periodic discoveries in the smaller emirates, Abu Dhabi will continue to dominate the oil scene in the UAE in terms of production and reserves. The emirate is continuing to make new finds, is discovering new structures in existing fields and has the ability to sustain relatively high levels of long-term production at its old fields by using improved recovery techniques. At the 2004 rate of production of 1,955,000 barrels per day (bpd), Abu Dhabi oil reserves give the emirate a reserve production ratio of 129 years.[1] In 2005, Abu Dhabi stepped up its crude oil output to 2.24 million barrels per day (mbpd), not counting some 250,000 bpd of condensate.[2]

The gas reserves of Abu Dhabi are presently estimated at 198.5 trillion cubic feet (tcf). In 2005, Abu Dhabi's natural gas production was 6.8 billion cubic feet/day.[3]

The UAE has extensive experience in terms of its relationships with foreign oil companies—the first oil concession was granted in Abu Dhabi in 1939. Certain aspects of this long experience; some of the decisions taken in the past; certain features of the applicable legal framework; and the history of Abu Dhabi's relationship with foreign oil companies are relevant to this study, and have therefore been included.

In the UAE, like the other countries of the Middle East, all natural resources, including underground petroleum resources, belong to the state. Article 23 of the UAE Constitution stipulates: "The natural resources and wealth in each emirate shall be considered to be the public property of that emirate. The public authority shall be responsible for the protection and proper exploitation of such natural resources for the benefit of the national economy."[4] Furthermore,

[2]

Article 1206 of the UAE Civil Transactions Code states: "Minerals found under the ground shall be the property of the State even if they are found in a privately owned land."[5]

The UAE has neither a unified federal oil policy nor any federal petroleum legislation under which the conditions governing the granting of exploration and development permits are fixed in advance. Each emirate handles its own petroleum affairs. While the UAE does have a Federal Petroleum Ministry, its present role is confined to representing the country in the international petroleum community and in specialized international and regional organizations such as OPEC, OAPEC and the Arab Organization of Mineral Resources. It is for these reasons that the UAE cannot be considered to have a unified legal framework for the development of petroleum resources.

Since Abu Dhabi is the largest oil-producing emirate, with the biggest oil reserves, the richest experience in the oil industry and the longest history of relationships with foreign oil companies, it is the most logical candidate among the emirates for a study of the legal framework for the development of petroleum resources and related experiences in this field.

Chapter 1 of this book describes the growth of the petroleum industry in Abu Dhabi, while Chapter 2 outlines the main features of the legal framework for the development of petroleum resources in the emirate.

In order to illustrate the way in which the oil industry is being run and how exploration and production of oil and gas are carried out in Abu Dhabi, Chapter 3 details the present organizational structure of the oil industry in Abu Dhabi, the respective roles of the relevant governmental authorities, the Abu Dhabi National Oil Company (ADNOC) and the other operating companies, while also highlighting their main achievements.

In view of the particularity of the gas industry it is necessary to devote a separate chapter (Chapter 4) to Abu Dhabi's experience in the field of gas, while Chapter 5 deals with the fiscal regime of oil and gas operations in the emirate.

Chapter 6 is dedicated to the important subject of the settlement of disputes between oil-producing states and the oil companies operating therein, while Chapter 7 explores the evolving relationships between the Abu Dhabi government and international oil companies, including certain recent developments. Finally, the study ends with a conclusion chapter (Chapter 8), which will provide an insight into the future of Abu Dhabi's oil industry.

1

The Growth of the Petroleum Industry in Abu Dhabi

The petroleum industry in the UAE is an integral part of the oil industry in the Middle East. Like the other major oil-producing countries in the region the UAE is a member of the Organization of the Petroleum Exporting Countries (OPEC), and like the other Arab oil producers it is also a member of the Organization of Arab Petroleum Exporting Countries (OAPEC).

The UAE is affected in its policies, practices and activities by the objectives, polices and decisions of both of these organizations. It is a member of the Gulf Cooperation Council (GCC) which also includes Saudi Arabia, Kuwait, Bahrain, Qatar and Oman and works towards consolidating the relationships between member countries and coordinating their policies and positions in a variety of different fields (political, economic, social, cultural, etc.).

Like the other players in the Middle East oil industry, the UAE has been affected, in terms of the rise and development of its national oil industry, by the same circumstances and events as the other producers of the Middle East and has undergone a similar evolution. It is therefore appropriate to begin with a brief description of the growth of the oil industry in the region to serve as an historical background to the study of the Abu Dhabi petroleum industry.

[5]

Historical Background: The Growth of the Middle East Oil Industry

Foreign oil companies developed – and until the 1970s – completely controlled petroleum operations in the Middle East under concessionary agreements reached with local governments. The concessionary agreements developed in the Middle East determined the rights and obligations of the concessionaires and governments. The terms of the agreements varied from one country to another, and even from one agreement to another in the same country, but in general they had a number of common features:[1] the agreements were granted for extremely long periods (the average lifespan of the four main concessions in Iran, Iraq, Kuwait and Saudi Arabia was 82 years) without any provision for possible modification; they covered very large areas of the host country (sometimes the total territory of the country concerned without specific provisions for relinquishment); before 1950 they provided for the payment to the host government of an extremely low royalty made at a fixed rate per ton—in the Abu Dhabi agreements, three rupees (75 cents) per ton (about 10 cents per barrel); and while the concessionaire company was granted exorbitant privileges and great managerial freedom in the development of the concession area, the host country was excluded from any direct participation in the internal decision making process of the operating companies. Finally, under the old concessionary system, the oil industry had been operated as a wholly foreign economic enclave, almost completely isolated from other sectors of the national economy.

The growing demand for petroleum in industrialized countries, combined with their lack of oil deposits, stimulated petroleum exploration in a number of distant regions. Several attempts were made even before the First World War to obtain rights for the use of oil resources in promising areas through concessionary agreements with local governments. The British businessman William D'Arcy obtained an important concession for oil exploration in Iran on May 28, 1901.

After the end of the First World War the struggle for control of the countries of the Middle East and their promising oil resources intensified between the United States and the European powers. The Europeans were anxious to control these countries after the collapse of the Ottoman Empire. Fearing the early exhaustion of their reserves, the Americans made a determined effort to obtain control of a considerable share of oil resources in promising areas, particularly in the Middle East.

Iraq witnessed a fierce struggle over the acquisition of oil concession rights by foreign interests. Although the British attempted to seize all the concession rights, they finally agreed under pressure from their war-time allies that a group of European and American interests be granted the much sought-after concession in Iraq and, later, in various other areas formerly constituting provinces of the Ottoman Empire. In Iraq the concession rights were effectively granted to the Turkish Petroleum Company in 1925, which was later to become known as the Iraq Petroleum Company (IPC).

In 1930 the US Bahrain Petroleum Company (BAPCO) obtained a concession for oil exploration in Bahrain; and in Saudi Arabia the Arabian American Oil Company (Aramco) obtained a concession covering the whole of Saudi Arabia in 1933. In the following year, a concession was granted by the Sheikh of Kuwait to the Kuwait Oil Company (KOC), which was equally owned by the Gulf Oil Corporation and the Anglo-Persian Oil Company (APOC). This was followed by the acquisition by the Iraq Petroleum Group of oil concessions in the Arab Emirates – known at the time as the "Trucial Sheikhdoms," where the first concession was granted in Abu Dhabi in 1939 – Oman and Qatar.[2]

The pattern of petroleum operations outside the United States, and particularly in the Middle East, that took shape in the interwar period based on the oil concessionary system, continued following the end of the Second World War with only minor changes in its underlying principles. This pattern was characterized by the emergence of a group of international oil companies – five American, one British, one British–Dutch and one French – which established virtual control over the world's major oil resources outside the United States and the Soviet Union. The seven large international oil companies, known as the "Seven Sisters" and joined later by Compagnie Française des Pétroles (CFP), agreed to divide among themselves the concession areas of the Middle East, and not to compete with each other.[3] These eight companies, also known as "the Majors" are shown below in Table 1.1.

The Majors engaged not only in the exploration of oil reserves and the production of crude petroleum, but became integrated companies in order to control most of their refining, transportation and marketing of oil. In most cases these companies established joint ventures, and were able to reach agreements with one another regarding production and marketing in defined areas.[4]

Table 1.1
International Oil Companies: "The Majors"

COMPANY	NATIONALITY
Standard Oil of New Jersey	US
Royal Dutch/Shell Group	British/Dutch
Gulf Oil	US
Texaco	US
Mobil Oil	US
Standard Oil of California (SOCAL)	US
British Petroleum (BP)	British
Compagnie Française des Pétroles (CFP)	French

Subsequent Changes in the Ownership and Control of the Oil Industry

The relationships between the producing countries of the region and the international oil companies, under the traditional oil concession system, underwent a series of changes in the 1950s, 1960s and 1970s. These successive changes led finally to the collapse of the traditional concession system and ultimately to state control over the oil industries in producing countries. In his excellent study entitled *OPEC and the International Oil Industry: A Changing Structure*, Fadhil Al Chalabi describes this process of structural change in the Middle East oil industry:

> This system of complete domination by the cartel of upstream investment and extraction operations lasted a long time and effectively remained fully operational until the early seventies. The developments which led eventually to the total collapse of the whole system, involved the radical changes of the last seven years, which brought about a complete reversal in oil investment relationships and eventually the replacement of the foreign companies in the ownership and management of the oil industry by the governments of the producing countries.[5]

The main factors, developments and events behind this radical change in the relationships between international oil companies and the producing countries of the Middle East were:

UN Resolutions on Permanent Sovereignty over National Resources

The most important of these resolutions was UN General Assembly (GA) Resolution No. 2158 of 1966, which "advised" host countries to exercise their permanent sovereignty, and to accelerate acquisition of full control over production operations as well as management and marketing. These resolutions provided considerable political and moral support to the growing complaints and claims made by Middle Eastern oil-producing countries.

The Establishment of OPEC (1960)

The main objectives of this institution when it was established were to defend the legitimate common interests of its members and present those members as a unified front of producers in their interaction with foreign oil companies. OPEC provided the members with collective bargaining power. In a few years it became a strong, unified force for advancing governmental aspirations with tangible achievements to its credit: it successfully resisted any lowering of the posted prices of crude oil; affected many substantial changes in favor of the producing countries in terms of the fiscal regime applicable to oil operations; and prompted some improvements in the structure of the oil industry. OPEC played a prominent role in introducing the principle of state "participation" in the industry and in incorporating it into the concession agreements of its member states.[6]

The Establishment of National Oil Companies

The establishment of national oil companies in certain countries of the Middle East was a significant step towards effective state participation in their respective oil industries. According to Al Chalibi:

> Perhaps the most significant development which contributed to the shake-up of the concession system, and which played a great role later on in radically changing the structure of the industry, was the growing trend in the producing countries towards the establishment of national oil companies. These were designed from the beginning to be the instruments through which the state could exercise its rights over national resources.[7]

The first national oil company in the Middle East was the National Iranian Oil Company (NIOC), which established during the dramatic nationalization of Iranian oil in 1951 by the government of Prime Minister Mohammed Mossadegh. Elsewhere, the Kuwait National Petroleum Company (KNPC) was established in 1960; the General Petroleum and Mineral Organization (PETROMIN) was established in Saudi Arabia in 1962; and the Iraq National Oil Company was established in 1965. The emirate of Abu Dhabi would wait until November 1971 to establish its Abu Dhabi National Oil Company (ADNOC).

Nationalization of the Oil Industry in the Middle East

Al Chalibi writes: "The attempt at nationalization made by the Mossadegh Government in Iran in the early fifties was the first world event which, despite its failure, had a far-reaching political impact on the concession system and which led to its first shake-up."[8]

In Algeria some independent US companies holding small concessions were seized by the government in 1967, and in December 1971 Libya nationalized the British Petroleum (BP) share in the joint venture with Bunker Hunt. Al Chalibi continues:

> However, the successful radical experiment in nationalization which completely reversed oil relationships in the Middle East ... was the nationalization by the Iraqi government of IPC (Iraq Petroleum Company Ltd., covering the northern fields) in the summer of 1972, followed by the nationalization of the Basrah Petroleum Company (covering the southern fields) which in turn led by 1975 to total nationalization of all Iraqi oil.[9]

New Investors in the Oil Industry of the Middle East

One of the major developments in the postwar period was the appearance on the international scene of oil companies outside the Majors and their entry to the oil industry in the producing countries. The Italian national oil company, Ente Nazionale Idrocarburi (ENI) was the pioneer in this respect, followed by the French Company Entreprise des Recherches et d'Activités Petrolières (ERAP) and the Japanese Petroleum Trading Company.

These companies concluded agreements with the governments of certain producing countries that were more favorable to those countries, in the form of joint ventures and service contracts. A number of American independent oil companies, like Occidental, Amoco and Pan American, also entered the industry. *The Arab Oil and Gas Directory 2005* notes:

> The entry of these new investors into regions dominated by the Cartel created a new situation that fed national aspirations to be rid of the multi-national companies' control and to resort to independent companies for securing technological expertise, crude oil marketing outlets and capital needs to meet investment risks.[10]

Participation in Existing Concessions

The concept of participation of the host countries in existing concessions gained increasing support among the major oil-producing countries in the 1960s and was soon to receive the blessing of the newly established forum of the oil producers—OPEC. The first formal approbation of OPEC came in 1968. Later, in September 1971, OPEC called on members to "establish negotiations to achieve effective participation." Negotiations effectively began in May 1972 between the producers (as a group) and a group of the oil companies, leading to the General Agreement on Participation which was signed in Riyadh on October 5, 1972. It was initially signed by Saudi Arabia and Abu Dhabi, followed by Qatar and Kuwait.

In view of the importance of participation – which represented a radical change in the oil industry of the Middle East – the subject will be dealt with later in some detail, outlining its main features and the practical manner in which it has been implemented in the Abu Dhabi oil industry (see Chapter 3).

Subsequent Takeovers in Some Countries of the Region

The Abu Dhabi government was content with a 60 percent participation arrangement. However, over time other countries in the area achieved a 100 percent takeover of the oil companies operating in their respective countries.

Kuwait announced on March 5, 1975 that as of that date it had taken over all the assets of the KOC. In February 1976, Kuwait began negotiations for the takeover of AMINOIL, which was operating in the neutral zone between Kuwait and Saudi Arabia, but when negotiations did not go as planned, Kuwait nationalized Aminoil in September 1977.

Starting in June 1976, Qatar negotiated the complete takeover of its concessionaires, signing broadly similar agreements with the Qatar Petroleum Company (QPC) in September 1976 and Shell in February 1977. Both companies agreed to continue operations under a management fee of 15 cents per barrel of oil produced.

In Saudi Arabia, the government purchased all the assets of Aramco in 1976, acquiring full ownership of its hydrocarbon reserves and oil industry facilities in their entirety. However, Aramco remained a company incorporated in the United States and the four US Majors that owned it continued to operate the assets on the Saudi government's behalf, producing, refining and exploiting crude oil and natural gas on a fee basis. They also pursued an active hydrocarbon exploration program.

Aramco finally became a Saudi-registered, state-owned concern in 1988, when its name was changed to the Saudi Arabian Oil Company (Saudi Aramco) and its head office moved to Dhahran. Saudi Aramco now has sole responsibility for all upstream operations in the Kingdom.[11]

Oil Production in the Middle East

Iran was the first of the major producers of the Middle East, with the discovery of oil at Masjid-i-Sulaiman in southern Iran in 1908 and the start of commercial production in 1912. Iranian production continued to expand until the nationalization of its petroleum industry in 1951. Between 1951 and 1954 Iran's oil production declined drastically, but after the settlement of the nationalization issue in October 1954, output resumed its upward trend.[12]

The second major producer of the region was Iraq, where a small field was discovered at Naft-Khaneh in 1923 and put into operation for local consumption. Next, a major field was discovered at Kirkuk in 1927, and subsequently another important field was struck at Ain Zalah. However, because these fields were so far inland, it was not until 1934 that oil production began in large quantities; oil flowed abroad after two pipelines were laid from Kirkuk to the Mediterranean ports of Haifa and Tripoli.

There was also large scale development of Iraq's southern oil resources, located near the Arabian Gulf, which resulted in the production and flow of crude oil in 1951. These developments increased Iraq's crude oil output from 30 million barrels in 1936 to 50 million in 1950 and 251 million in 1955.

In 1938, petroleum reserves were discovered in Saudi Arabia at Dammam and subsequently at Abqaiq, while the outbreak of the First World War retarded the development of the oil fields of Kuwait and Qatar. The large-scale development of the petroleum industry undertaken in these areas in the postwar years, as well as in the neutral zone lying between Kuwait and Saudi Arabia, facilitated a sharp growth in crude oil production—in Kuwait from the Borgan and Magwa fields and in Saudi Arabia from the Abqaiq and Ghawar fields. The crude oil output of Saudi Arabia rose from 8 million barrels in 1944 to 456 million in 1960; Kuwait's output increased from 6 million barrels in 1946 to 594 million in 1960; and Qatar's output rose from 12 million in 1950 to 64 million in 1960.[13]

Table 1.2 shows world and Middle East oil production in selected years during the period from 1930 to 1958. The table illustrates the rapid increase in production and the rising percentage of the Middle East share of world oil production, reaching 23.66 percent in 1958.

Table 1.2

World and Middle East Oil Production (selected years)

Year	World Production (tons)	Middle East Production (tons)	Middle East Share of World Production (%)
1930	195,000,000	6,340,000	3.3
1935	225,000,000	11,490,000	5.0
1940	289,000,000	13,900,000	4.8
1945	356,000,000	26,550,000	7.5
1948	465,000,000	56,910,000	12.2
1950	518,000,000	86,600,000	16.8
1951	582,000,000	96,190,000	16.5
1952	605,000,000	104,440,000	19.0
1953	654,000,000	121,620,000	20.1
1954	681,000,000	136,000,000	20.0
1955	768,790,000	162,468,000	21.26
1956	841,650,000	172,549,000	20.90
1957	882,200,000	177,900,000	20.20
1958	905,200,000	214,300,000	23.66

Source: Benjamin Shwadran, *The Middle East, Oil and the Great Powers 1959* (1959), 441

Already in 1959, Benjamin Shwadran, in *The Middle East, Oil and the Great Powers 1959* stressed the increasing importance of Middle East oil to the world oil industry: "The Middle East as an oil-producing region as well as an area of great reserves has become increasingly significant in the last fifteen years." He remarked that the region's oil reserves were estimated, in 1954, at 56 percent of the world's oil reserves, adding: "Not only in estimated reserves, however, but also in actual production the Middle East has emerged in the last dozen years as an important factor in the world oil markets." He concludes his remarks by stating: "Since 1950 the Middle East has become the major single supplier of oil in the international market."[14]

Similarly, Stephen Longrigg, in his authoritative book *Oil in the Middle East: Its Discovery and Development*, stresses the significance in the late 1960s of oil reserves and production in the Middle East by stating: "In the matter of proved reserves the region holds unshakably its dominating position; it possesses more than 60% of the world's discovered and available stocks." He concludes: "The main task of providing the world with the next century's demand for energy, that is, for fuel, seems therefore ineluctably to belong to the Middle Eastern Oilfields ... Proved oil reserves are by far the greatest in the world, oil containing structures extraordinarily large and productive, individual and average production per well remarkably high."[15]

The continued importance of Middle Eastern oil reserves and production throughout the twentieth century and early twenty-first century, is illustrated in Tables 1.3 and 1.4, both published by OPEC. Table 1.3 shows world proven crude oil reserves by region (1970–2005), while Table 1.4 shows world crude oil production by region for the same period. Both tables testify to the ongoing importance of the Middle East in terms of oil reserves and production. The emirate of Abu Dhabi continues to be one of the major players in the region's petroleum industry.

Table 1.3
World Proven Crude Oil Reserves by Region, 1970–2005 (Million Barrels)

	1970	1971	1972	1973	1974	1975	1976	1977	1978	1979	1980	1981
North America	49,751	46,511	46,539	44,724	43,650	39,782	37,142	35,486	33,804	36,610	36,611	35,409
Latin America	26,171	30,486	31,368	29,458	30,548	36,072	32,573	40,223	41,489	57,130	74,033	84,187
Eastern Europe	61,014	58,796	55,921	52,339	59,341	61,878	62,900	62,000	61,438	62,878	65,800	65,695
Western Europe	6,926	9,626	10,555	17,490	25,726	25,640	24,858	27,595	24,415	23,837	22,761	22,333
Middle East	336,221	346,377	350,046	349,951	403,358	387,071	380,169	376,766	370,715	362,655	362,910	365,244
Africa	51,107	54,635	59,487	61,569	60,479	59,086	55,019	53,718	52,884	53,221	52,468	56,354
Asia and Pacific	17,262	24,853	25,105	27,123	31,424	33,313	35,614	34,890	35,747	33,202	33,391	33,864
Total world	548,452	571,284	579,022	582,654	654,526	642,842	628,275	630,678	620,491	629,534	647,973	663,085
OPEC	399,436	410,973	417,171	419,326	482,168	463,051	453,560	447,876	443,134	435,556	434,614	438,312
OPEC percentage	72.8	71.9	72.0	72.0	73.7	72.0	72.2	71.0	71.4	69.2	67.1	66.1

	1982	1983	1984	1985	1986	1987	1988	1989	1990	1991	1992	1993
North America	34,547	34,168	34,415	34,176	32,829	33,169	32,959	32,401	31,839	29,974	28,838	27,993
Latin America	89,527	90,716	92,884	118,529	119,119	121,915	121,957	121,499	122,746	125,506	130,183	131,362
Eastern Europe	65,384	65,255	64,662	64,233	62,135	60,370	59,788	59,592	58,568	58,534	58,953	58,932
Western Europe	21,340	21,985	22,579	22,067	19,822	17,188	17,846	16,892	16,890	16,950	17,385	17,877
Middle East	388,592	397,053	431,006	431,428	537,184	566,768	655,830	663,348	662,019	662,461	663,307	663,485
Africa	57,877	57,309	56,255	56,200	57,265	57,063	57,839	58,023	58,599	59,943	60,842	60,906
Asia and Pacific	33,919	35,395	36,322	37,059	37,141	37,895	38,049	33,452	34,047	35,030	35,160	36,260
Total world	691,185	701,881	738,123	763,691	865,495	894,369	984,265	985,206	984,708	988,398	994,667	996,814
OPEC	467,371	475,295	509,998	535,798	643,016	674,020	760,484	764,830	765,879	771,947	773,702	774,541
OPEC percentage	67.6	67.7	69.1	70.2	74.3	75.4	77.3	77.6	77.8	78.1	77.8	77.7

	1994	1995	1996	1997	1998	1999	2000	2001	2002	2003	2004	2005
North America	27,356	27,245	26,856	27,477	25,911	26,469	26,901	27,101	27,167	27,200	26,591	26,071
Latin America	131,340	132,473	138,792	140,886	123,836	125,714	122,234	124,595	117,529	117,045	118,680	118,364
Eastern Europe	58,968	58,961	64,783	64,791	71,131	74,550	76,976	78,848	87,408	90,433	91,629	93,660
Western Europe	19,786	20,990	18,540	18,751	18,348	18,885	19,251	19,410	18,403	18,038	17,392	16,967
Middle East	665,766	665,394	675,946	676,600	677,606	678,537	694,579	698,638	730,102	735,083	739,136	742,688
Africa	63,636	70,972	73,542	73,862	76,222	84,303	93,380	96,892	102,064	112,430	113,573	117,774
Asia and Pacific	35,702	35,539	35,678	36,660	38,789	38,903	39,521	40,322	38,551	38,344	38,125	38,439
Total world	1,002,553	1,011,574	1,034,137	1,039,028	1,031,844	1,047,360	1,072,841	1,085,807	1,121,226	1,138,574	1,145,125	1,153,962
OPEC	777,400	785,066	802,819	805,967	810,264	818,247	840,538	847,884	881,679	890,714	896,659	904,255
OPEC percentage	77.5	77.6	77.6	77.6	78.5	78.1	78.3	78.1	78.6	78.2	78.3	78.4

Source: OPEC Annual Statistical Bulletin 2005.

Table 1.4
World Crude Oil Production by Region, 1970–2005 (1,000 b/d)

	1970	1971	1972	1973	1974	1975	1976	1977	1978	1979	1980	1981
North America	10,963.4	11,010.7	11,061.1	10,950.3	10,408.9	9,755.3	9,387.0	9,507.6	9,956.7	9,945.3	9,891.0	9,730.2
Latin America	5,174.9	5,069.4	4,837.8	5,141.2	4,800.5	4,294.6	4,339.8	4,537.4	4,765.4	5,267.0	5,574.5	5,949.9
Eastern Europe	7,411.2	7,802.6	8,223.9	8,814.4	9,564.4	10,227.8	10,750.3	11,321.9	11,810.2	12,066.5	12,388.6	12,528.9
Western Europe	469.5	444.0	462.4	472.5	485.7	637.3	921.1	1,431.4	1,792.2	2,334.0	2,518.7	2,728.5
Middle East	13,779.4	16,163.9	17,941.5	21,052.6	21,705.2	19,438.3	22,046.7	22,223.4	21,122.7	21,568.8	18,345.1	15,556.3
Africa	6,032.1	5,689.7	5,684.1	5,888.0	5,382.0	4,944.6	5,893.9	6,276.5	6,065.7	6,584.3	6,061.1	4,642.2
Asia and Pacific	1,544.0	1,907.0	2,381.8	2,924.6	3,298.0	3,696.5	4,111.0	4,555.6	4,726.3	4,990.5	4,916.7	4,851.7
Total world	45,374.6	48,087.2	50,592.5	55,243.6	55,644.6	52,994.5	57,449.7	59,853.7	60,239.2	62,756.3	59,695.7	55,987.7
OPEC	23,300.1	25,208.0	26,891.1	30,629.5	30,350.7	26,771.1	30,327.1	30,848.1	29,394.8	30,511.3	26,501.5	22,183.2
OPEC percentage	51.4	52.4	53.2	55.4	54.5	50.5	52.8	51.5	48.8	48.6	44.4	39.6

	1982	1983	1984	1985	1986	1987	1988	1989	1990	1991	1992	1993
North America	9,775.6	9,857.6	10,148.8	10,221.8	9,809.8	9,586.8	9,419.7	8,836.3	8,562.4	8,611.7	8,406.8	8,143.0
Latin America	6,238.2	6,116.0	6,174.3	6,097.6	6,059.0	6,068.8	6,114.2	6,346.6	6,871.6	7,134.0	7,270.8	7,350.8
Eastern Europe	12,636.3	12,699.5	12,605.9	11,986.3	12,309.1	12,448.4	12,367.7	12,037.7	11,275.9	10,140.6	8,844.5	7,922.2
Western Europe	2,988.9	3,357.3	3,696.8	3,853.1	3,930.9	4,064.4	4,046.3	3,896.2	4,098.4	4,317.1	4,559.3	4,823.0
Middle East	12,929.7	11,149.8	10,518.3	9,724.8	12,102.9	11,920.0	14,149.9	15,133.7	16,076.9	15,892.1	17,563.1	18,264.5
Africa	4,403.2	4,442.5	4,609.0	4,871.1	5,149.5	4,789.0	4,949.4	5,541.6	5,961.6	6,212.2	6,324.7	6,166.9
Asia and Pacific	4,622.8	4,798.4	5,251.2	5,531.9	5,750.2	5,744.3	5,854.4	6,004.3	6,269.5	6,417.6	6,362.7	6,462.5
Total world	53,594.6	52,421.1	53,004.4	52,286.5	55,111.4	54,623.7	56,901.7	57,796.4	59,116.4	58,725.3	59,331.9	59,133.0
OPEC	18,734.4	16,615.6	15,933.7	14,921.0	17,660.2	16,741.5	18,841.4	20,406.3	22,021.1	22,249.2	23,845.1	24,230.5
OPEC percentage	35.0	31.7	30.1	28.5	32.0	30.6	33.1	35.3	37.3	37.9	40.2	41.0

	1994	1995	1996	1997	1998	1999	2000	2001	2002	2003	2004	2005
North America	8,012.3	7,939.8	7,865.8	7,865.7	7,679.4	7,227.1	7,213.1	7,178.8	7,191.3	7,140.1	6,823.9	6,480.0
Latin America	7,556.3	7,721.2	8,148.0	8,476.2	9,467.4	9,122.9	9,316.5	9,327.4	9,491.2	9,573.2	9,967.6	10,206.5
Eastern Europe	7,168.6	7,050.3	6,930.8	7,093.0	7,083.3	7,212.0	7,624.6	8,243.4	9,036.5	9,953.6	10,733.9	11,098.1
Western Europe	5,585.9	5,812.0	6,181.1	6,202.2	6,109.1	6,176.9	6,287.5	6,033.6	5,949.6	5,626.7	5,372.9	4,904.4
Middle East	18,808.5	18,856.3	19,012.3	19,603.7	21,115.6	20,283.2	21,415.4	20,776.6	18,649.1	20,439.0	22,001.7	22,783.6
Africa	6,121.2	6,199.6	6,419.4	6,589.8	6,705.0	6,351.8	6,771.1	6,620.9	6,449.0	7,276.3	8,347.9	8,856.7
Asia and Pacific	6,630.7	6,833.8	7,025.6	7,123.1	7,049.9	7,109.1	7,251.5	7,211.5	7,279.7	7,274.3	7,330.3	7,433.5
Total world	59,883.5	60,412.9	61,583.0	62,953.7	65,209.7	63,483.0	65,879.7	65,392.2	64,046.4	67,283.2	70,578.2	71,672.9
OPEC	24,609.4	24,600.8	24,769.2	25,431.8	27,739.7	26,227.8	27,745.0	26,873.5	24,322.5	26,884.6	29,549.2	30,673.3
OPEC percentage	41.1	40.7	40.2	40.4	42.5	41.3	42.1	41.1	38.0	40.0	41.9	42.7

Source: *OPEC Annual Statistical Bulletin 2005*.

Note: Totals may not add up, due to independent rounding. Revisions have been made throughout the time series.

The Rise of National Oil Companies in the Middle East[16]

National oil companies in the producing countries of the Middle East were created in order to meet the aspirations of those countries for "permanent sovereignty" over their national resources; to provide them with an appropriate instrument for securing more direct national involvement in their petroleum industries; and as a reaction to the dominant position of the Majors under the old-style concessions.

When the underdeveloped countries of the Middle East gained – or consolidated – their political independence in the post-Second World War period, their economic independence remained incomplete. It was clear to these states that without economic independence a comprehensive plan for economic development based on their natural resources could not be implemented. Regarding the exploitation of their main natural resource, petroleum – the source of 60–95 percent of the revenues of each country – these states realized that this field was fully dominated and controlled by foreign concessionaires operating under the old-style concession agreements.

UN Resolutions on Permanent Sovereignty

Underdeveloped countries' desire for economic independence, coupled with their frustration with the major oil concessions (and similar forms of agreements covering other national resources in some countries) prompted these countries to raise the issue of permanent sovereignty over natural resources at the United Nations as early as 1952. "The United Nations was asked to play a major role in helping developing countries to attain their economic independence, a role similar in scope and importance to that of granting political independence to colonies and non-self-governing territories."[17]

The concerted efforts of the underdeveloped countries led to the issuance of a series of UN resolutions on the question of permanent sovereignty over national resources. The first resolution was passed in 1952, followed by a series of further resolutions that emphasized the right of the state over its own resources, culminating in UN GA Resolution 2158 of 1966, which was even more explicit in defining the rights of host countries. Host countries were "advised" to secure the maximum exploitation of natural resources by exercising their permanent sovereignty through accelerated acquisition of full control over production operations, managing and marketing. Host countries were also urged "to secure and increase their share in administration of enterprises which are fully and partly operated by foreign capital."[18]

Improvements in the Concession Terms

The producing countries of the Middle East, equipped with this new concept of economic rights endorsed by the highest international forum, pursued efforts to introduce improvements in the terms and conditions of concession agreements. Certain improvements in the terms of the original concessions were effectively achieved in the 1950s and 1960s, mainly in the financial fields (e.g., the introduction of the 50–50 profit sharing formula and the principle of "expensing of royalty") to cope with the changing situation but the basic features remained unchanged, due to the adamant resistance of the concessionaries, particularly to the concept of government control. Where governments could not alter the agreements to their satisfaction in the concession areas, they were at least able to opt for a more appropriate form of development in the new acreage which was available to them—either because they were not originally covered by the concessions or were subsequently relinquished by the concessionaries. An appropriate method open to the host governments would have been to pursue a course of sole development. Yet in the 1950s and 1960s few of the producing countries were in a position to develop that acreage alone because they either lacked the risk capital, required technology, markets, etc. or even the institutional framework in the form of experienced national oil companies to undertake such development. The need was therefore felt – for the first time in some of the concerned countries – for national involvement in the oil industry, not to replace the major concessionaries but to work alongside the Majors in whatever areas were open to them and acquire experience in the different phases of the oil business.

It was at this stage that the model of the "joint venture agreement" was conceived in order to provide a compromise on the issue of how to maintain permanent sovereignty over natural resources while simultaneously developing them. The first model of this form of agreement was introduced to the region in 1957 when ENI, under Enrico Matei, signed joint venture agreements with Egypt and Iran. This model allowed the government to retain privileges and operational control over a foreign oil company, thereby putting it on an equal footing with the concessionary partner. This also helped to integrate the oil industry into the national economy and develop local skills.

The Establishment of National Oil Companies

Having adopted, or at least contemplated this new model of economic development of their oil resources, the governments of the oil-producing countries of the Middle East soon realized the necessity of creating publicly-owned, semi-autonomous corporations to hold the national share in joint ventures with foreign interests. To ensure the success of such entities it was recognized that they should be free from administrative rigidities, able to exercise a reasonable measure of independence in decision-making and be operated as commercial companies in terms of their management and accounts. This decision prompted the creation of a number of national companies in the region. Even those countries which were not pursuing joint ventures in the immediate future decided that they too should establish their own national companies to ensure some measure of direct involvement in future ventures. The idea of national companies was attractive, quickly gained ground and ultimately developed into a trend.

To underdeveloped countries rich in oil resources, the Italian state-owned ENI (established in 1953) represented an attractive model of a public oil corporation. By its success in Italy, ENI proved that a national oil company could effectively compete with foreign interests in the development and marketing of national resources.

ENI was established on February 10, 1953 by a takeover of the enterprises which had been created or acquired by the state in the field of hydrocarbons. The oldest of the state enterprises put under ENI's control was AGIP Mineralia, which was set up in 1926 by the state with the objective of carrying out petroleum exploration and processing operations. After the Second World War, with Enrico Mattei as chairman of AGIP's board, the functions of the state-owned enterprise expanded as a result of the discovery of important oil and natural gas fields, principally in the Po Valley. Thereafter, various private Italian concerns and international oil companies filed applications with the government for exploration permits in the Po Valley. The government decided not to grant any permits for petroleum exploration and development but to entrust these operations to a state-owned entity. In the Act of Establishment of ENI, the publicly-owned corporation received the exclusive right to explore for and develop the Po Valley hydrocarbon reserves, including the right to process and market the oil and gas produced.

Vigorous exploration and development programs led to a swift increase in gas output from the Po Valley. ENI's activities soon spread, in competition with foreign oil companies, to cover all phases of the oil and gas industry, covering the rest of the Italian mainland and islands. In 1962, the ENI group comprised 72 companies.[19]

As mentioned earlier, the first national oil company to be formed in the Middle East was the National Iranian Oil Company (NIOC), which was established during the nationalization of the Iranian oil industry in 1951 by the government of Mohammed Mossadegh in order to take over the operation of nationalized fields. After the attempt to nationalize Iranian oil, NIOC survived and was later made a party to a consortium agreement concluded in 1954 with a group of international oil companies that replaced the Anglo-Iranian Oil Company. That agreement assigned to NIOC the responsibility for non-basic operations in the concession area. The company had to wait several years to see its activities extended to cover "basic" operations (outside the scope of the consortium) by virtue of the Iranian Oil Act of 1957 which stipulated in its first article that NIOC represented the state in planning and executing oil policies in the best interests of the country.

Although the other oil-producing countries of the region were similarly dissatisfied with the prevailing status of the exploitation of their oil resources, they dismissed the option of implementing similarly radical measures. Instead, they chose to achieve their goals in a gradual fashion. Regarding new acreage in particular, governments found the appropriate solution in the emerging model of joint venture agreements, which led to the creation of national oil companies through which they could exercise their sovereignty and control over their petroleum resources outside the areas of the major concessions and alongside foreign concessionaries.

The Kuwait National Petroleum Company (KNPC) was established along these lines in 1960, followed in 1962 by the General Petroleum and Mineral Organization (PETROMIN) in Saudi Arabia, and in 1965 by the Iraq National Oil Company. Furthermore, it is interesting to note that Venezuela, a major oil-producing country in the western hemisphere, also established its national oil corporation, Corporación Venezolana del Petróleo (CVP), in that same period (April 1960).

The establishment of national oil companies in the states of the Middle East was a significant step towards their effective participation in their oil industries. However, those states were far from satisfied with the marginal activities and modest role played by their national companies while the major concessionaires continued to dominate their oil production.

Inevitably, therefore, the existing concessions came under increasing pressure in the mid-1960s. At the time, policy makers in most of the states concerned did not support the growing demands for full nationalization. Therefore, an alternative strategy became a political necessity. This alternative was found in the concept of participation in existing oil concessions, which would not only present an opportunity for the host country to share the management of the oil operations under the main concessions, but would enable these operations to become more integrated into the local economy.

The concept of participation gained increasing support among the major oil producers and was soon to receive the blessing and the collective approbation of OPEC. The first formal approbation by OPEC came in July 1968, when the 16th OPEC Conference passed Resolution XVI.90 which endorsed the policy of reasonable participation for host governments in existing concessions. In July 1971, the 24th OPEC Conference passed a further resolution,

XXIV.135, which called upon all member states to "take immediate steps towards the effective implementation of the principles of participation." This was followed in September 1971 by Resolution XXV.139 which called on members to begin negotiations to achieve effective participation. Negotiations started in May 1972 between the Majors and Saudi Arabia, Qatar, Abu Dhabi and Kuwait that led to the General Agreement on Participation which was initialed in Riyadh, on October 5, 1972. It was signed by Saudi Arabia and Abu Dhabi on December 20, 1972, by Qatar on January 4, 1973 and by Kuwait on January 8, 1973.

As the entry of the host governments into the participation arrangements with the concessionaires required the existence of a corporation to hold the national share and to exercise its role in the operations, those countries without national oil companies were called upon to establish them. Abu Dhabi's oil production did not reach significant levels until the late 1960s (in 1967 its total crude oil production reached 382 kbpd), before which the establishment of a national company was considered unnecessary. After 1969 Abu Dhabi began to examine the idea of establishing a national oil company like the other oil producers in the region. Ultimately, with the move towards participation and in anticipation of the role which it would assume under a participation agreement, the Abu Dhabi National Oil Company (ADNOC) was established by virtue of Law No. 7 of November 27, 1971.

Common Objectives of National Oil Companies

Since their establishment, national oil companies have developed and expanded their role through different methods and with varying degrees of success. However, the general objectives, common to all national oil companies in the region, can be summarized as follows:

- To act as the arm of the state apparatus entrusted with implementation of its overall petroleum policy in conformity with both its development objectives and those of the operating companies which are responsible for executing approved projects.
- To enable the state to acquire greater direct experience in all phases of the oil industry and to promote the creation of an independent integrated national industry covering as wide a range of oil activities as possible, both within the country and abroad.
- To hold the state's share in the operating companies and play the role of the national partner in participation arrangements and joint ventures, thereby exercising more effective control over the activities of the operating companies through participation in the decision-making processes and directing and monitoring activities in the interests of the host country.

A Profile of the Petroleum Industry of Abu Dhabi[20]

Oil exploration in the emirate of Abu Dhabi began in 1939 when a 75-year exploration and production concession was granted by the ruler of the emirate, Sheikh Shakhbut bin Sultan Al Nahyan, to Petroleum Development (Trucial Coast) Limited – PD(TC) – a subsidiary of IPC (the name of the company was later changed to the Abu Dhabi Petroleum Company Ltd. – ADPC – in 1962). Ownership shares in PD(TC) were as follows: AIOC 23.75%, Royal Dutch/Shell Group 23.75, CFP 23.75%, Standard Oil of New Jersey and Mobil Oil 23.75% and Partex 5%. The concession covered the whole of the emirate's land and marine territories as well as its islands. Initial geological surveys began soon after the concession was granted, but were interrupted by the outbreak of the Second World War. Activities resumed in 1947.

Initial Onshore Exploration and Production

The first onshore well was drilled in 1950 in the Ras Al Sadr area, but was abandoned. Drilling resumed in 1958 in the Bab area and oil was discovered. Owing to the encouraging results produced by the first four wells drilled, it was decided to develop the Bab field which came on stream in 1962. While the development of the Bab field was underway, work began on the construction of a 113 km, 61 cm pipeline to a site at Jebel Dhanna, northwest of the field, which was chosen as the most suitable loading terminal. Work on the pipeline and terminal was completed in 1963 and the first cargo of Bab crude was shipped at the end of the year.

After the discovery of oil in the Bab field and the conclusion of exploratory work, oil was discovered at Bu Hasa in 1962. Oil was also discovered in one of four wells drilled in the Asab region. Subsequently two extensions of the Asab field were proven, one to the south named Shah, and the other named Sahil to the north. The Asab field came on stream in 1973, after the drilling of five producing wells which were linked to the pipeline system to Jebel Dhanna by a 200 km, 61 cm pipeline from Asab to Habshan.

Following the discovery of the Bab and Asab fields, ADPC started to relinquish parts of its original concession to the government in 1965. By the end of 1976, the company's total concessionary area was reduced to around 32,000 km^2, all onshore.

During the 1970s, ADPC's efforts were directed primarily towards the maintenance of the total productive capacity of the three main onshore fields – Bab, Bu Hasa and Asab – which reached 1.28 million barrels per day (mbpd) in 1973–74.

Main Onshore Oil Fields:

- **Bab:** This field was discovered in 1953 and by 1958 its potential had been established. The Bab field is located 80 km southwest of Abu Dhabi city. The field is 45 km long, 25 km wide and has an area of about 120 km^2. It produces a high quality 39–40° API crude. In 1974 its average rate of production was already 100,000 barrels per day (bpd), and its production capacity was subsequently increased.

- **Bu Hasa:** This field, which lies some 80 km southwest of Bab and 160 km southwest of Abu Dhabi city was discovered in 1962. The field is 35 km long and 19 km wide. Work on its development began at the beginning of 1964 and in 1965 it was connected to the export terminal at Jebel Dhanna. By 1974, Bu Hasa was producing 500,000 bpd from 37 wells whose production rates varied between 6,500 and 40,000 bpd.

- **Asab:** This field, which lies 225 km south of Abu Dhabi city, was discovered in 1965 and development began during the second half of 1971. Initial production at the beginning of 1974 was 460,000 bpd from 28 producing wells. Asab field is 25 km long, 10 km wide and has a surface area of 250 km^2. It produces a high quality 40° API crude.

Initial Offshore Exploration and Production

Intensive offshore exploration in Abu Dhabi started in 1953 when a 65-year exploration and production concession was granted by Sheikh Shakhbut to the D'Arcy Oil Exploration Company Ltd. The concession only covered Abu Dhabi's marine territory, including all submerged lands over which Abu Dhabi exercised sovereignty, except for the territorial waters and islands already covered by the PD(TC) – later to become the ADPC – concession.

Abu Dhabi Marine Areas Limited (ADMA) was established on May 18, 1954. Initially, two-thirds of ADMA was owned by BP and one-third by CFP, and the D'arcy concession was transferred to it on March 22, 1955. Later, in 1972, BP sold 45 percent of its shares in ADMA to the Japan Oil Development Company (JODCO).

As a result of various survey tests, ADMA was successful in locating several promising geologic structures. The first offshore well was drilled in 1958 on the crest of the Umm Shaif structure, around 97 kilometers from the mainland and in a water depth of 18.3 meters. The well produced 40° API oil in one limestone zone and natural gas in another.

Because of the company's belief that the Zakum structure was less important than Umm Shaif, the drilling of its first well at Zakum was delayed until April 1963. After drilling down to 3558.8 meters, oil was discovered in the Thamama zone and gas in the Araej zone.

In further exploratory drilling between 1962 and 1964, ADMA discovered the small Bunduq field on the Qatar–Abu Dhabi territorial waters boundary. ADMA then discovered a number of new but relatively small fields, including the Abu Al Bukhoosh field north of Umm Shaif on the boundary with Iran.

Following demarcation of the offshore areas between Abu Dhabi and Qatar in 1970, the Bunduq company was established – with a shareholding of one-third each by BP, CFP and the United Petroleum Development of Japan group – to develop and operate the Bunduq field which came on stream in 1976. Revenues from this field, which produced 20,000 bpd in 1977, have been shared equally between Abu Dhabi and Qatar.

Subsequently, another company, Total Abu Al Bukhoosh, was established to develop and operate the Abu Al Bukhoosh field which came on stream in 1974.

On December 6, 1967, a 45-year offshore concession was granted to Abu Dhabi Oil Co. (Japan) Ltd. (ADOCO) in an area relinquished by ADMA. The company is owned by a consortium of Japanese companies. On May 4, 1969 the company commenced drilling its first well on the Mubarraz structure and struck 33°API oil in the Thamama formation with a production rate of 3,000 bpd.

In 1976, ADOCO's rate of production was raised to 23,000 bpd. After the collection of crude produced from the wells on the principal production platform, it was pumped to Mubarraz island (about 16 km west of Abu Dhabi City) where storage facilities and a small export terminal were constructed.

Main Offshore Oil Fields:

- **Umm Shaif Field**: This field, which has a surface area of about 400 km^2, lies 153 km northwest of Abu Dhabi city and 35 km northeast of Das Island. The Development of this field began in 1960 and the field was put on stream in mid-1962. A 45.7 centimeter submarine pipeline with a total length of around 35 km was laid from Das Island to the west where a gas separation station, a crude treatment unit, storage facilities and a loading terminal were built. The first tanker load of Umm Shaif crude was exported on July 4, 1962. The field's output during that month averaged around 25,000 bpd. This initial rate of production was subsequently increased to 100,000 bpd in 1971.

- **Zakum Field**: The Zakum field has a surface area of roughly 910 km^2 and lies about 80 km northeast of Abu Dhabi city. The Zakum field was found to contain oil in two productive formations known as Upper Zakum and Lower Zakum, all within Lower Cretaceous Thamama limestone. Initially, Lower Zakum was chosen for development because of its higher reservoir pressure. The field was put on stream in 1967 and linked to Das Island terminal by a 90 km, 76.2 cm submarine pipeline. The development of Upper Zakum was entrusted in 1977 to the Zakum Development Company (ZADCO), one of ADNOC's affiliates.

- **Das Island**: Das Island is a small island (2.4 km long and 1.2 km wide), 161 km northwest of Abu Dhabi city. In addition to being the main oil gathering, processing, storage and export terminal for ADMA and the Bunduq Company, the Abu Dhabi Gas Liquefaction Company (ADGAS) has a large plant on the island for the liquefaction of natural gas from the Zakum and Umm Shaif fields. Total storage capacity on the island is about 7.1 million barrels. The storage tanks are connected to the island's two fixed and one floating oil-loading berths which are capable of handling very large crude carriers (VLCCs).

Oil and Gas Reserves and Production

Crude Oil Reserves

According to one study, at the beginning of 1974, Abu Dhabi ranked fourth among the Arab oil producers and fifth among OPEC countries in terms of its proven oil reserves, which were estimated at 30 billion barrels. The three main fields of Umm Shaif, Zakum and Bu Hasa were among the largest 68 fields in the world—with reserves exceeding 1 billion barrels.[21] However, a reliable source in 1977 already put the estimate of Abu Dhabi's recoverable reserves at the much higher figure of 66 billion barrels.[22]

New discoveries made since then and the use of more advanced techniques in the industry have pushed the estimate of Abu Dhabi's proven oil reserves to a much higher figure—many reliable sources in the industry put the most recent figure at 92.2 billion barrels.[23]

One industry source states: "The UAE is sitting on the world's sixth largest oil reserves."[24] Furthermore, other reliable sources in the industry estimate UAE oil reserves to be around 97.8 billion barrels. This estimate has not changed since the early 1990s. Out of these reserves, around 95 percent (or about 92.2 billion barrels) lie beneath the emirate of Abu Dhabi.[25]

Table 1.5, prepared by OAPEC, shows the oil reserves in the Arab states during the period 2000–2005. According to this table, the UAE ranks fourth after Saudi Arabia, Iraq and Kuwait.

Table 1.5
Oil Reserves in Arab Countries, 2000–2005 (billion barrels)

	2005	2004	2003	2002	2001	2000	
UAE	97.8	97.8	97.8	97.8	97.8	97.8	الإمارات
Bahrain	0.1	0.1	0.1	0.1	0.1	0.2	البحرين
Tunisia	0.3	0.3	0.3	0.3	0.3	0.3	تونس
Algeria	11.4	11.4	11.8	11.3	11.3	11.3	الجزائر
S.Arabia	264.3	264.3	262.7	262.8	262.7	262.8	السعودية
Syria	3.2	3.2	3.2	3.2	3.2	2.5	سورية
Iraq	115.0	115.0	115.0	115.0	115.0	112.5	العراق
Qatar	15.2	15.2	15.2	15.2	15.2	13.2	قطر
Kuwait	101.5	101.5	99.0	96.5	96.5	96.5	الكويت
Libya	39.1	39.1	39.1	36.0	36.0	36.0	ليبيا
Egypt	3.7	3.7	3.7	3.7	3.7	3.7	مصر
OAPEC	651.6	651.6	648.0	641.9	641.8	636.7	مجموع الأوابك
Sudan	6.3	0.8	0.8	0.8	0.8	0.3	السودان
Oman	5.5	5.6	5.6	5.7	5.9	5.9	عمان
Morocco	0.0	0.0	0.0	0.0	0.0	0.0	المغرب
Yemen	4.0	4.0	4.0	4.0	4.0	4.0	اليمن
Other Arab Countries	15.8	10.4	10.4	10.5	10.7	10.1	الدول العربية الأخرى
Total Arab Countries	667.4	662.0	658.3	652.4	652.5	646.8	اجمالي الدول العربية

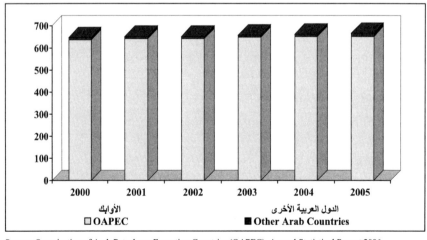

Source: Organization of Arab Petroleum Exporting Countries (OAPEC), Annual Statistical Report 2006.

[32]

Natural Gas Reserves

"The United Arab Emirates has one of the largest gas reserves in the world, ranking next to the Soviet Union and Iran." This statement was made in 1977 by the then UAE Minister of Oil and Mineral Resources. He added: "Abu Dhabi contains large reserves of natural gas both onshore and offshore and produces more than 90% of all the gas produced in the UAE."[26]

It is known that natural gas is produced either in association with crude oil, in which case it is referred to as "associated gas," or separately from independent gas fields, known as "non-associated gas" or "cap gas."

According to sources in the industry, estimates of the natural gas reserves in the emirate of Abu Dhabi put them between 198.5 trillion cubic feet, and 196.1 trillion cubic feet (in the period between 2002 and 2005).[27] According to some sources, the total gas reserves of the UAE are estimated at 6,010 billion cubic meters of which around 91.4 percent are in Abu Dhabi.[28] The most recent estimate available puts Abu Dhabi's proven natural gas reserves at 5,620 billion cubic meters as of January 1, 2006, representing about 93 percent of the UAE's total gas reserves of 6,043 billion cubic meters.[29]

Table 1.6, also prepared by OAPEC, shows the natural gas reserves in Arab countries for the period 2000–2005. The UAE, according to this table, ranks third among Arab countries after Qatar and Saudi Arabia in terms of its natural gas reserves.

Table 1.6
Natural Gas Reserves in Arab Countries
2000–2005 (billion cubic meters)

	2005	2004	2003	2002	2001	2000	
UAE	6071	6060	6060	6060	6060	6003	الامارات
Bahrain	92	92	92	92	92	110	البحرين
Tunisia	78	78	78	78	78	78	تونس
Algeria	4545	4545	4545	4523	4523	4455	الجزائر
S.Arabia	6848	6834	6754	6646	6456	6146	السعودية
Syria	371	371	371	371	371	241	سورية
Iraq	3170	3170	3170	3190	3109	3109	العراق
Qatar	25783	25783	25783	25783	25783	11152	قطر
Kuwait	1586	1572	1572	1557	1557	1557	الكويت
Libya	1491	1491	1491	1503	1314	1274	ليبيا
Egypt	1897	1854	1725	1657	1557	1444	مصر
OAPEC	51932	51850	51641	51460	50900	35569	مجموع الأوابك
Jordan	6	6	6	7	7	7	الأردن
Sudan	113	85	85	85	85	85	السودان
Oman	829	849	849	829	859	859	عمان
Morocco	1	1	1	1	1	3	المغرب
Yemen	479	479	479	453	396	396	اليمن
Other Arab Countries	1428	1420	1420	1375	1348	1350	الدول العربية الأخرى
Total Arab Countries	53360	53270	53061	52835	52248	36919	اجمالي الدول العربية

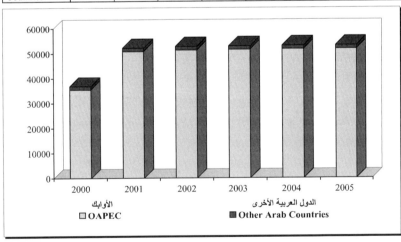

Source: Organization of Arab Petroleum Exporting Countries (OAPEC): Annual Statistical Report 2006.

Oil Production

As mentioned previously, oil production in Abu Dhabi commenced offshore in 1962 (Umm Shaif field) and then onshore in 1963. According to a report released by Middle East Economic Consultants (MEEC), from 1962 to 1977 "Abu Dhabi's oil production and the volume of its exports increased at an average annual rate of 48 percent. This is undoubtedly one of the highest rates of growth achieved in any of the oil-producing countries."[30] Table 1.7 shows Abu Dhabi's total exports and total production of crude oil for the period 1962–1977 from onshore and offshore fields. The table shows that in that period, the greater part of Abu Dhabi's crude oil was produced from onshore fields (Bab, Bu Hasa, Asab and Sahil).

Table 1.7
Abu Dhabi Production and Exports of Crude Oil
1962–1977 (in 1,000 barrels)

Year	Production			Exports
	Onshore	Offshore	Total	Total
1962	-	5,998	5,998	-
1963	649	17,591	18,240	18,060
1964	46,795	22,436	69,232	67,803
1965	69,727	33,168	102,895	102,096
1966	93,180	38,099	131,279	132,494
1967	94,092	45,076	139,168	137,560
1968	115,196	67,165	182,361	181,446
1969	129,897	88,901	218,798	218,824
1970	155,093	98,140	253,233	253,534
1971	209,859	131,118	340,977	338,562
1972	222,919	161,258	384,177	384,212
1973	288,718	186,898	475,616	472,113
1974	335,020	180,116	515,139	511,702
1975	327,108	186,226	513,334	514,071
1976	375,131	205,359	580,489	577,465
1977	373,984	228,782	602,765	596,285

Source : UAE Ministry of Petroleum and Mineral Resources.

Table 1.8 shows Abu Dhabi's oil production from onshore and offshore fields and oil exports for the period 1990–2003. The table shows that in some recent years (e.g., 1995 and 2002) Abu Dhabi overall production was supplied almost equally from onshore and offshore fields.

Concerning the oil production capacity of Abu Dhabi, while the emirate was able to step up oil production in 2004 when output rose to 1.96 mbpd (from around 1.9 mbpd in 2003), it still had over 500,000 bpd of spare capacity. The emirate's operators, however, continue to increase oil production capacity both onshore and offshore, since the Abu Dhabi Supreme Petroleum Council (SPC) has set a target of boosting total capacity to 2.85–3 mbpd by 2006 and 3.7 mbpd by 2010.[31] There are no reports to confirm that the target figure for 2006 has been achieved, but according to one source the production capacity rose to 2.7 mbpd in the second quarter of 2006.[32]

Table 1.8

Abu Dhabi's Oil Production and Exports (kbpd)

Year	Total	Onshore	Offshore	Exports
1990	1,716	774	942	1,544
1995	1,788	950	838	1,573
1997	1,950	960	990	1,683
2000	1,990	1,015	975	1,770
2002	1,690	850	840	1,450
2003	2,000	1,050	950	1,760

Source: Abu Dhabi National Oil Company (ADNOC)

Table 1.9, prepared by OAPEC, shows oil production in the Arab countries for the period 2000–2005. The table ranks the UAE second among the Arab countries in this period (after Saudi Arabia) in terms of its crude oil production.

Table 1.9
Production of Crude Oil in Arab States (kbpd)

	2005	2004	2003	2002	2001	2000	
UAE	2468	2344	2287	1900	2231	2280	الامارات
Bahrain	175	174	190	186	182	181	البحرين
Tunisia	72	70	66	72	70	74	تونس
Algeria	1350	1311	1111	850	842	796	الجزائر
S.Arabia	9443	8897	8410	7093	7890	8090	السعودية
Syria	450	503	528	508	522	547	سورية
Iraq	1840	2106	1328	2127	2600	2700	العراق
Qatar	800	755	635	568	632	648	قطر
Kuwait	2428	2289	2107	1746	1947	1984	الكويت
Libya	1640	1581	1428	1316	1324	1347	ليبيا
Egypt	696	709	750	751	760	768	مصر
OAPEC	21361	20739	18839	17117	19000	19416	مجموع الأوابك
Jordan	0	0	0	0	0	0	الأردن
Sudan	290	287	255	230	230	193	السودان
Oman	765	783	819	897	956	955	عمان
Morocco	0	0	0	0	0	0	المغرب
Yemen	350	350	448	435	436	437	اليمن
Other Arab Countries	1405	1420	1523	1562	1622	1585	الدول العربية الأخرى
Total Arab Countries	22766	22159	20361	18680	20622	21000	اجمالي الدول العربية

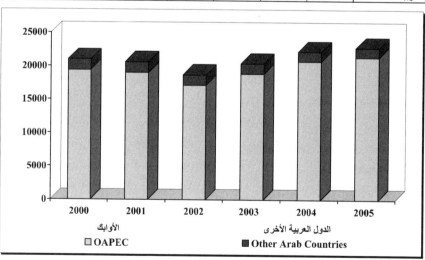

Source: Organization of Arab Petroleum Exporting Countries (OAPEC).

[37]

Natural Gas Production

Until the second half of 1977, when gas exports commenced, most of the gas produced in Abu Dhabi was flared. Between 1974 and 1976, for example, approximately 12 percent of the associated natural gas produced annually from onshore fields, and around 26 percent of that produced offshore was utilized—mainly in pumping stations and power generation in the fields, and in the case of onshore gas, in electricity and water distillation plants in Abu Dhabi city. This is compared with an estimated US$1 billion worth of associated natural gas that was flared over the period 1973–1977.[33]

This situation began to change with the promulgation of Law No. 4 of 1976 on Abu Dhabi's ownership of natural gas, the commencement of production from the gas liquefaction plant on Das Island in 1977 and the establishment of Abu Dhabi Gas Industries Limited (GASCO) in 1978.

Downstream Operations

Downstream operations in the oil industry are the operations that follow the discovery and production of crude oil. Oil is said to flow downstream from well-head to gas station. These operations cover the refining and processing of oil and gas, transportation by pipeline or tanker, local distribution of refined products and marketing.

The petroleum industry of Abu Dhabi covers all phases of the industry, including all downstream activities. Since these activities are carried out by ADNOC and its affiliates and subsidiaries, they shall be dealt with in Chapter 3.

To conclude this profile of the petroleum industry of Abu Dhabi, the following is a quote from a statement made by ADNOC on its website:

> The UAE's proven oil reserves now stand at around 98 billion barrels, representing just under 10 percent of total world oil reserves. This places UAE as the fourth largest OPEC producer,

after Saudi Arabia, Iran and Venezuela. Abu Dhabi's proven oil reserves have doubled in the last decade and now account for 94 percent of the UAE's total oil reserves. This is the result of significantly increasing the rate of recovery, continuing to identify new finds, especially offshore, and discovering new oil-rich structures in existing fields.

ADNOC's oil production capacity has risen to over 2 million barrels per day, ranking it among the top 10 oil producers in the world. This has been achieved through major investments in a number of recent and ongoing development projects.

These include a $300 million project to increase capacity of the onshore Bu Hasa field to 480,000 b/d, a natural gas re-injection project for the onshore Bab field, and a $480 million project to increase capacity of the Ruwais refinery from 145,000 to 500,000 b/d. These form part of the overall goal of raising the UAE's production capacity to 3 million b/d by 2006.[34]

2

The Legal Framework for the Development of Petroleum Resources

There exists no comprehensive petroleum legislation in Abu Dhabi, although certain aspects of the petroleum industry are covered by specific legislation. Three pertinent laws may be cited in this respect: the Abu Dhabi Income Tax Decree of 1965, as amended; Law No. 8 of 1978 on the Conservation of Petroleum Resources; and Law No. 4 of 1976 on the emirate of Abu Dhabi's ownership of gas. The legal framework for the development of petroleum resources is, therefore, determined by the terms and conditions of the individually negotiated oil agreements concluded between the government and foreign oil companies. These agreements have taken various forms over the years and have passed through different stages of evolution since the granting of the original old-style concessions.

The Original Concession Agreements and their Evolution (ADPC Onshore 1939; ADMA Offshore 1953)

As in other oil-producing countries in the Middle East, the development of petroleum resources in Abu Dhabi was governed by old-style concession agreements from the discovery of oil until the early 1970s, when "participation" arrangements were concluded.

In the post-Second World War period, the producing countries of the Middle East made significant efforts to improve the terms and conditions of the concession agreements. Some improvements were effectively achieved in the 1950s and 1960s, mainly in the financial area—examples being the introduction of a 50–50 profit sharing formula in the early 1950s; changes adopted by OPEC agreements, e.g., expensing of royalty[1] in 1964–1965; and the rise in the income tax rate applicable to oil companies from 50 percent to 55 percent in 1970–1971. Besides these financial changes, the overall characteristics of the concessions remained unchanged until the introduction of the participation concept in the early 1970s.

The efforts of OPEC members to improve the financial terms of the major oil concessions continued until 1974, when an income tax of 85 percent and a royalty of 20 percent were introduced. This has been known ever since as the "OPEC Formula."

Abu Dhabi's first concession agreement, between Sheikh Shakhbut of Abu Dhabi and PD(TC), was signed in January 1939 (the company was renamed Abu Dhabi Petroleum Company – ADPC – in 1962). The duration of the concession was 75 years and it covered the entire combined onshore and offshore area of Abu Dhabi. Following preliminary exploration, the company relinquished the offshore areas but kept all the onshore areas. Production of oil began under this concession in 1963.

Abu Dhabi's second major concession was granted in 1953 to ADMA and covered all of the emirate's offshore areas for a duration of 65 years. Production began under the offshore concession in 1962. Oil exploration and exploitation in Abu Dhabi was governed for many years by these two main old-style concessions.

In 1966 the government and the two concessionaires agreed to replace the fixed royalty of three rupees per ton with a royalty of 12.5 percent and the two companies agreed to submit to the Income Tax Law of 1965, paying income tax at the rate of 50 percent.

Concessions Granted in the Period 1967–1971

While the government of Abu Dhabi, like the other oil-producing counties of the Middle East, exercised every effort to improve the terms of the old-style concessions, it simultaneously continued to work towards concluding new agreements with better terms and conditions covering the acreage relinquished by the major concessionaires. With the support of OPEC and having gained political and economic independence and acquired better knowledge of the various aspects of the oil industry, the emirate concluded new agreements on more favorable terms. The entry of independent oil companies into national petroleum industries was encouraged in order to put an end to the complete dependence of the host countries on major oil companies. Independent oil companies offered better terms and new conditions that were instrumental in the revision of the old agreements.

Beginning in 1967, Abu Dhabi concluded a number of new agreements, maintaining the legal form of the concession system, but with significant improvements. The first set of these agreements was concluded in the period 1967–1971 and a second in the period 1980–1981 with still further improvements.

Mana Al Otaiba, former Minister of Petroleum and Mineral Resources of the UAE, summarizes the features of the new concession agreements that distinguished them from the old-style concessions:

- *Elimination of duress and monopolistic features.*
- *Elimination of exclusivity*: In the new agreements each company is allocated a limited area of the host country's territory.
- *Introduction of relinquishment obligations.*
- *Reduction of the concession period*: While old agreements allowed for long periods extending to 75 years, in the new agreements this has been reduced, sometimes to between twenty and twenty-five years.

- *Improved financial terms*: In addition to the payment of bonuses and rentals, in varying amounts, the host country now receives – on the discovery of oil – a royalty which can go up to 20 percent, plus income tax at a rate that can reach 85 percent. Moreover, the oil companies are obliged to spend specified minimum amounts annually on exploration and drilling.
- *Incorporation of the principle of participation*: The host country is now given the option, on discovery of oil in commercial quantities, to acquire a share in the capital of the operating company varying between 50 percent and 80 percent.
- *Priority of employment to nationals of the host country.*
- *Industrialization of the host country*: The new agreements provide not only for the processing of oil and gas locally but also for the establishment of industry in the host country by extending financial and technical aid.[2]

Al Otaiba concludes:

[I]t will be clear from the foregoing that the new concession agreements which were concluded after the advent of political independence in the host countries did away with the undesirable privileges of the old agreements. Further, the new agreements opened the door for the entry of the independent oil companies and for the host countries to be offered better terms as a result of the competition created amongst the oil companies.[3]

Commercial quantities of oil were discovered in the concession areas covered by three of these new agreements concluded in the period 1967–1971:

- **Abu Dhabi Oil Company (Japan) Limited (ADOC)**

This company was granted an offshore concession on December 6, 1967, for a period of 45 years. In addition to standard provisions on payment of bonuses and annual rentals, the company paid an expensed royalty of 12.5 percent plus income tax at 55 percent of its net profits (this rate was raised in 1971 from 50 percent). The concession provided the government with the option, on discovery of oil in commercial quantities, to acquire 50 percent of the company's shares.

- **Total Abu Al Bukoosh Company**

This company was awarded a concession in July 1973 covering the Abu Al Bukoosh field which was originally part of the ADMA concession and had since been relinquished. In 1974, the government received taxes from the company at the rate of 55 percent in addition to a royalty of 12.5 percent. In 1975, these were raised to 65 percent and 16 percent respectively.

- **The Bunduq Company Ltd.**

This company was set up in July 1970 to develop the Bunduq field which traverses the marine boundary between Abu Dhabi and Qatar. It undertook to develop this field on behalf of the two countries, with the profits being shared equally between them. The governments of Abu Dhabi and Qatar agreed to collect an income tax of 75 percent and a royalty of 20 percent and allowed the company an amortization period of five years.

The oil production from these three companies was relatively small when compared with that of the two major concessions granted to ADPC and ADMA. However, these agreements did have a symbolic value as they represented a concrete improvement in aspects of their basic features when compared to the old-style concessions. They therefore represented a step forward towards the satisfaction of the host country's objectives and put pressure on the major oil companies holding the old concessions to satisfy some of the interests and claims of the host country.

Significantly, the government never exercised, in any of these newer concessions, its option to acquire equity in the company upon the discovery of oil in commercial quantities.

Participation Agreements in the Period 1972–1974

One of the most important privileges granted to the original concessionaire companies was their almost absolute authority in controlling and managing the oil operations of the host countries. Although the producing countries in the area succeeded in introducing certain improvements in these concession agreements – especially in the financial field – the concessionaires continued to retain complete freedom in policy making and were able to disregard the host countries' demands to share important decisions regarding their oil operations. Therefore, no room was left for host governments or their national companies to be involved in oil-related activities.

Inevitably, the concessions came under increasing pressure beginning in the mid-1960s. As policy-makers in most of the countries concerned refused to support – at the time – the growing demands for nationalization, an alternative strategy was becoming a political necessity. This alternative was found in the concept of participation in the existing oil concessions, presenting an opportunity for the host country to share in the management of the oil operations under the main concessions rather than being confined to marginal activities.

A general agreement on participation was signed in December 1972 between governments in the region (Saudi Arabia, Abu Dhabi, Qatar and Kuwait) and the oil concessionaires in these countries. This agreement took effect at the beginning of January 1973. National companies were entrusted to hold and manage the governments' share in the participation agreements. The initial share of participation granted was 25 percent, which meant that the governments were entitled to a corresponding share of the production. The actual share of production left to the government was, however, effectively much reduced through many devices, such as those related to *phase-in* and *bridging* oil.[4]

The General Agreement on Participation defined only the general principle, with the understanding that each country would conclude a detailed implementing agreement with its concessionaires. Soon thereafter the governments concerned realized that this initial participation arrangement – with a low percentage share of 25 percent – was inadequate, especially as actual management was, in effect, left in the hands of the foreign companies, which remained majority shareholders. These governments, including Abu Dhabi, therefore decided to immediately negotiate an increase in their participation share. In Abu Dhabi, two agreements were concluded in September 1974 – with each of the major concessionaires, ADPC onshore and ADMA offshore – raising Abu Dhabi's participation to 60 percent. This arrangement was effective retroactively from the beginning of 1974.

In view of the importance of these 1974 participation agreements, which continue to provide the framework for the relationship of the Abu Dhabi government with international oil companies, Chapter 3 will provide an outline of their main features and an assessment of the practical manner in which they are implemented.

The Most Recent Concession Agreements: 1980–1981

Starting in late 1980, Abu Dhabi awarded a number of new concessions to foreign companies, with the aim of encouraging such companies to spend up to US$1 billion on exploration in the period up to 1988. Six of these concessions were awarded during 1980–81.

Some of the earlier concessions awarded in the 1960s to companies such as Philips, Aminoil, Agip and a Japanese consortium headed by Mitsubishi in areas relinquished by ADPC, had been abandoned.[5] In October–November 1980, four new onshore blocks were awarded. The first went to Amoco, the second to a Canadian group headed by Sceptre Resources, while the third and fourth were both awarded to a consortium led by Amerada Hess, which included Occidental and Alpha Oil.

The next phase came in 1981 when a consortium led by Deminex of West Germany was awarded a 35-year concession in offshore areas. Later in that year a further offshore block was awarded to Attock Oil.

Since these concessions comprise the most up-to-date model of oil agreements concluded by Abu Dhabi, they deserve special attention and careful analysis. These agreements follow a standard format with standard basic terms and conditions. They are examples of what has become known in oil industry literature as a "modern license regime" or "modernized concession agreement."[6] The Deminex Agreement concluded on May 3, 1981 was chosen for study as it is representative of the latest model of concession agreement adopted by Abu Dhabi.

Although this form of agreement has not been mandated by legislation as being the imperative model to follow (as in those countries with comprehensive petroleum legislation to which is attached a model agreement), it has undeniable significance in that, being the latest agreement, one can expect it to be followed in the future until a new model of agreement is adopted, dictated by circumstances.

The Deminex Agreement[7]

In the Agreement, the government granted exclusive rights to the company to explore, search and drill for, then produce, store, transport and sell petroleum within the concession area (Article 2). The terms of the Agreement cover a period of 35 years from the effective date (Article 4).

It is worth noting that the duration of this Agreement, although shorter than the term of some earlier agreements concluded in the period 1967–1971 (some of which went up to 45 years), is still relatively long compared to the current trend in OPEC member countries. For example in Algeria the agreements last from 17 to 23 years. In Qatar the duration of the most recent agreements with Sohio and Amoco (1985/1986) is 25 years and in Iran it is 20 years. Furthermore, the Agreement does not distinguish between the duration of the various phases of petroleum operations, i.e., exploration, development and production.

Article 3, entitled "Ownership of Natural Gas," stipulates that "All natural gas that may be discovered or produced in the concession area in association with crude oil or independently shall be subject to the provisions of Law No. 4 of 1976."[8] Law No. 4 of 1976 established Abu Dhabi's sole ownership over all its associated and non-associated gas.

Article 6 spells out the obligations of the concessionaire and specifies the minimum sums to be spent on drilling and development in each of the first eight years:

Article 6 – Work Obligations

A. The company shall within six (6) months of the effective date commence to explore for petroleum and shall within eighteen (18) months after the effective date complete initial geophysical operations in the concession area for the purposes of assessing the prospects of the area for production of petroleum.

B. The company shall within two (2) years after the effective date commence drilling a test well. Having commenced a test well the company shall proceed with due diligence in accordance with good oilfield practice to completion thereof and to completion of any other test well or wells which it may at any time thereafter drill in the concession area; provided, however, that in no event shall the aggregate depth of such well or wells be less than thirty thousand (30,000) feet (hereinafter referred to as "Minimum Depth Requirement") unless crude oil is discovered in commercial quantities before reaching the "Minimum Depth Requirement" whatsoever in the drilling of any well or wells in the concession area.

C. The company shall undertake to spend on prospecting, exploration, drilling or development operations, even though petroleum may have been discovered in commercial quantities, the following minimum amounts: ... [These amounts increase gradually from $2.5 million in the first year to $8 million in the eighth year].

D. If the expenditure in any year shall be less than the amounts specified above for such year, the company shall expend the deficiency during the next succeeding two years in addition to the amounts specified for those years. In the event that the expenditure in any year shall be greater than that required for such year, such excess shall be credited against expenditure obligations for any succeeding year or years.[9]

Article 10 provides for bonus payments—an initial bonus of US$2 million upon commercial discovery, $5 million after regular exports of crude oil have reached an average of 100,000 bpd and $10 million after regular exports have reached 200,000 bpd.

Article 11 provides for annual rentals and Article 12 covers relinquishment. In view of the basic improvements introduced by the Article concerning the topic of relinquishment, the full text of the Article appears below:

A. (i) The company shall relinquish to the government not less than 25 percent of the non-productive portion of the concession area within three years from the effective date and shall further relinquish another 25 percent of the non-productive portion of the concession area within five years from the effective date and shall further relinquish another 25 percent of the non-productive portion of the concession area within eight years from the effective date.

(ii) The Company may at any time relinquish to the government all or any part of the concession area upon giving three months' notice in writing of their intention to do so. Any area relinquished under this sub-paragraph shall count towards the company's obligation under sub-paragraph (i) above.

B.   The portions so relinquished shall so far as is reasonably possible be a block or blocks of sufficient size and convenient shape, taking into account contiguous areas already relinquished and not the subject of a further concession to enable oil operations to be carried out thereon.

C.   The notice of relinquishment shall be accompanied by a map and a description indicating the precise extent of the land to be relinquished and the land to be retained.

D.   Upon relinquishment, the portions so relinquished shall cease to be of the concession area and the provisions of Article 30 hereof shall apply thereto, but the company shall continue during the duration of this agreement to enjoy the right to use the portions so relinquished for transport and communications facilities and to do so in a manner which shall interfere as little as practicable with any use to which the relinquished portions may be put.

E.   If the company gives notification of relinquishment of the whole of the concession area and the company has not fulfilled the minimum investment obligation under paragraph (C) of Article 6 hereof then the company shall pay to the government a sum equal to one half of the under expenditure,[10] due prior to such notification, provided that the investment obligation in respect of the year in which such notification is given shall be reduced by the amount thereof apportioned on a daily basis referable to the period after the date of such notification.[11]

Article 13 deals with royalty payments and adopts the concept of a progressive or sliding-scale royalty whereby the company must pay the government a (fully expensed) royalty equal to 12.5 percent of the posted price of crude oil produced each year. If production during a calendar year reaches an average rate of 100,000 bpd, the company must pay a royalty of 16 percent. The royalty increases to 20 percent if production reaches an average rate of 200,000 bpd.

Article 14, entitled "Conservation and Natural Gas" stipulates the following:

A. The company shall be required to conduct its operations in accordance with the best conservation practices, bearing in mind the long-term interests of Abu Dhabi. To this end, the government shall draw up instructions detailing the conservation rules to be followed generally by the company within the concession area.

B. Natural gas produced by the company as a result of operations under this agreement shall be conserved to the maximum extent possible in the circumstances and in the best manner consistent with the accepted methods and standards of the petroleum industry and shall be flared only to the extent which is consistent with practices generally followed in the petroleum industry.

C. The company shall make best possible use of associated gas. Any associated gas which is not utilized by the company shall be the property of the government at source and the government shall be entitled to take such associated gas and make such use of it as it may wish in accordance with Article 3 of this agreement.[12]

Article 17 addresses taxation and adopts a sliding-scale of income tax. It stipulates that the company shall pay a basic income tax at a rate of 55 percent. However, if the production of crude oil during a calendar year reaches an average of 100,000 bpd, the company must pay income tax at a rate of 65 percent. If production reaches an average of 200,000 bpd the company must pay income tax at a rate of 85 percent.

For the assessment and payment of income tax the company is subject to the provisions of the Abu Dhabi Income Tax Decree of 1965 as amended and supplemented by the provisions of Article 17 of the agreement.

After having determined the taxation to which the concessionaire is subject, Article 18 of the agreement adds that no other or higher taxes, duties, fees or charges shall be imposed upon the company. This will be discussed in more detail in Chapter 5, which focuses on the applicable tax regime.

Under Article 19, the company is entitled to import, free of customs and other import duties, all materials needed to conduct operations. This also applies to the export of all petroleum produced.

Article 24 stipulates the priority of employment for nationals and other Arabs, and Article 26 deals with the training program the company is required to implement for its national employees.

Article 27 deals with information the company should provide the government on a regular basis to keep it fully informed as to the progress of all the company's operations.

Article 34, entitled "Amendments," embodies a classic clause in concession agreements according to which "the mutual consent of the government and the company shall be required to annul, amend or modify the provisions of this agreement." This clause is what many analysts in the field of oil agreements describe as a *protective* or *stabilization* clause. The validity and, more importantly, the effectiveness of such clauses are presently controversial issues.

Article 35 covers "Arbitrations." In view of the importance of dispute settlement clauses in oil agreements and the originality of the provisions of this Article, the full text is quoted below:

A. if any doubt, difference or dispute shall arise at any time between the parties hereto concerning the interpretation hereof or anything herein contained or in connection herewith, or concerning the rights and liabilities of any of the parties hereunder, and if the parties fail to settle it in any other way the same shall be referred to two arbitrators, one of whom shall be chosen by each party, and to a referee who shall be chosen by the two arbitrators within sixty (60) days of being requested to do so in writing by either party.

B. Each party shall nominate its own arbitrator within sixty (60) days after the delivery of a request so to do by the other party, failing which its arbitrator may at the request of the other party be designated by the President of the International Court of Justice. In the event of the arbitrators failing to agree upon a referee, the President of the International Court of Justice may appoint a referee, at the request of the arbitrators or either of them.

C. The decision of the arbitrators or, in the case of a difference of opinion between them, the decision of the referee, shall be final and binding on both parties.

D. The decision shall specify an adequate period of time during which the party against whom the decision is given shall conform to the decision and that party shall be in default only if that party has failed to conform to the decision prior to the expiry of that period and not otherwise.

E. The place of arbitration shall be Abu Dhabi or elsewhere at the discretion of the referee.

F. The referee shall determine the procedure of the arbitration being guided generally by the relevant rules of procedure established by Articles 32–69 inclusive of the Rules of the International Court of Justice of May 6th, 1946.

G. This Agreement shall have the force of law. It shall be given effect and shall be interpreted and applied in conformity with the principles of law normally recognized by civilized states in general including those which have been applied by international tribunals.[13]

This article warrants certain remarks:

- Paragraph B entrusts the President of the International Court of Justice to appoint a referee, in the case of failure of the two parties to agree, and Paragraph F states that the referee, in determining the procedure of the arbitration, shall be guided generally by the relevant rules of procedure of the International Court of Justice. These provisions carry connotations of an "international" dimension to the agreement or dispute.

- Paragraph G gives the agreement the force of law. This is a classic clause since the time of the old-style concessions. Its effectiveness is presently contested by some students of oil agreements, who believe that such a clause cannot transform the nature of the contractual provisions into statutory rules.[14]

- Paragraph G also stipulates that the governing law should be "the principles of law normally recognized by civilized states in general including those which have been applied by international tribunals." This is also a classic clause about which some authorities in this field have reservations. They highlight the present difficulty of reaching consensus on those general principles of law applicable throughout the world to all kinds of relationships between investors and host countries.[15]

Article 38, entitled "Better Terms," provides for a form of adaptation clause or a "most favored nation clause" in the following terms:

> If, in the future, arrangements are made between the government of Abu Dhabi and any other states in the Middle East or the agent of such a government and the company or any other company/companies operating in the petroleum industry as a result of which an increase in benefits should accrue generally to all such governments as aforesaid, then the government and the company shall review and discuss the changed circumstances within the petroleum industry in order to decide whether any alteration to the terms of this agreement would be equitable to both parties.[16]

Article 44 provides for government options to acquire, at any time after the discovery of oil in commercial quantities, a participating interest of up to 60 percent in all rights and obligations under the agreement. It then determines, in paragraph (B), the basis of calculating the payment to be made by the government for such participation:

> B. The government shall pay for such participating interest a sum equal to sixty (60) percent or such lesser proportion as the government shall have elected to acquire of the total accumulated costs and expenses recorded in the books of the company or of the operating company as the case may be as at the date of discovery of crude oil in commercial quantities (excluding the bonus and rentals paid by the company before the date of discovery of crude oil in commercial quantities).

The company shall notify the government within a period of forty five (45) days from the date of discovery of crude oil in commercial quantities of the total amount of such accumulated costs and expenses in order to enable the government to ascertain the sum it will have to pay if an election under this Article is made. The government shall have the right to appoint auditors to examine the said books and records of the company and of the operating company and to verify the said sum on its behalf. Payment of such sum shall be made by the government in ten equal installments together with interest on the outstanding balance at a rate equal to the prevailing rate of discount for the time being of the Federal Reserve Bank of the United States of America plus one percent, calculated from the date six months after the date of discovery of crude oil in commercial quantities. The first such payment shall be made at one (1) year intervals thereafter. If the government acquires a participating interest in this agreement pursuant to this Article, operations shall be conducted in accordance with the terms of the operating agreement to be concluded between the government and the company.[17]

According to the final part of this clause, if the government decides to acquire a participating interest in the venture, the text of the operating agreement is to be agreed upon after the government has exercised this option. Other agreements concluded by countries in the region have adopted a different approach—the basic principles of the operating agreement are agreed upon at the time of concluding the concession agreement and are appended to it in the form of an annex.

According to Article 45 entitled "Investment," when the production of crude oil reaches 100,000 bpd for a period of 90 days, the company must carry out – or prepare to conduct – studies as to the feasibility of carrying on one or more of the hydrocarbon processing activities specified in the Article.[18] The company must then execute the project for which the feasibility has been established. As part of the Agreement the company also undertakes to invest at least 10 percent of its profits in one or more of the projects whose economic viability has been established.

These are the main features of the new set of concessions awarded by the Abu Dhabi government in the early eighties. This model of concession agreement does not constitute a significant departure from those concessions awarded in 1967–1971—the basic terms are similar but certain improvements have been made, e.g., the duration is now 35 years (in the previous concessions it could be as much as 45 years); a progressive tax and royalty scheme has been adopted; an express clause has been incorporated covering government ownership of any gas discovered and the obligations of the concessionaire in this respect; work obligations are more substantial and bonuses and rentals are higher. Ultimately, although changes have been made, certain clauses could still be further improved to benefit the host country.

On the other hand, this last model of concession constitutes a real departure from the old-style form of concessions in that it eradicates the main drawbacks and disadvantages of that form of oil agreement—the very large areas allocated, the long duration of the concession, the modest financial benefits to the state and, most significantly, the complete exclusion of the state from any involvement in the oil operations, any equity shareholding and any participation in the decision-making process. It also satisfies most of the major demands of the host country, including its authority to exercise some review of, and control over the concessionaire's decisions: for example by requiring minimum exploration work programs; approval of the exploration costs and expenses and of field development plans; and by providing for a government option to participate in the venture.

The Legal Framework for Gas Development

As previously mentioned, the legal framework for the development of petroleum resources is determined essentially by the terms and conditions of the individually negotiated agreements concluded between governments and international oil companies.

The old-style concession agreements used to grant such companies the exclusive rights to explore for, develop and dispose of "petroleum," defined as including liquid as well as gaseous hydrocarbons. Consequently, host countries had no control over the gas associated with the production of oil.

Under contemporary participation agreements, however, producers now enjoy much greater authority and control over the concessionaire's oil operations. The wastage of associated gas by international companies is no longer an issue since the development and production of gas is generally excluded from the scope of the agreements. In the case of Abu Dhabi this was accomplished by Law No. 4 of 1976, the provisions of which are incorporated into the relevant contracts.

Law No. 4 of 1976 established Abu Dhabi's sole ownership over its associated and non-associated gas resources located in the emirate (see Appendix I). The main provisions of the law are:

Article 1

All gas which is already discovered or will be discovered in the territory of the Emirate of Abu Dhabi and which is recovered or produced from oil and gas wells in the Emirate, shall be solely owned by the Emirate of Abu Dhabi. The territory of the Emirate of Abu Dhabi shall include its land, territorial water and continental shelf ...

Article 4

Abu Dhabi National Oil Company shall have the right to exploit and use all quantities of gas referred to in Article 1 of this Law as well as the right to handle all other matters related to such gas. All rights acquired through oil agreements concluded by the Government of the Emirate of Abu Dhabi in connection with discovered or produced gas or with the facilities for the recovery and production of gas, shall devolve to Abu Dhabi National Oil Company.

Article 5

All oil companies operating in the Emirate of Abu Dhabi shall deliver all gas produced from oil and gas fields to Abu Dhabi National Oil Company in accordance with such conditions and technical arrangements as may be laid down by Abu Dhabi National Oil Company after consultation with such companies.

Article 6

Abu Dhabi National Oil Company shall have the right to exploit the gas referred to in Article 1 of this Law either on its own or through agreements or joint ventures concluded with other parties. In the latter case, the share of Abu Dhabi National Oil Company shall not be less than 51 percent of the capital.[19]

Law No.4 provides the government, through ADNOC, complete control over the exploitation of gas within its territory. ADNOC is responsible under this law for pursuing the interests of Abu Dhabi and for handling all matters relating to such gas. ADNOC is therefore entitled to arrange for the exploitation of gas resources either alone or through joint ventures with others, on acceptable terms and conditions, provided it retains a minimum shareholding of 51 percent in any joint venture. One of the legal consequences of this law is that ADNOC becomes the only supplier of gas feedstock for gas projects and ADNOC is entitled to a "gas payment" for all quantities of gas delivered to the gas joint ventures. Abu Dhabi's gas experience will be dealt with in more detail in Chapter 4.

The Governmental Authority in Charge of Petroleum Affairs

According to the UAE constitution, the natural resources in each emirate are the public property of that emirate and each emirate is entrusted with the development and exploitation of its own resources. The individual emirates have jurisdiction over their petroleum affairs. While the UAE does have a federal Petroleum Ministry, its role is confined to representing the country in the international petroleum community.

Before the establishment of the UAE federation in 1971, the emirate of Abu Dhabi was considered an independent state and had a Council of Ministers (one of whom was the Minister of Petroleum and Mineral Resources). This situation continued for some time after the establishment of the federation until the promulgation of Abu Dhabi's Law No.1 of 1974, concerning the "Re-organization of Government Machinery in the Emirate of Abu Dhabi." According to Article 1 of this Law, an Executive Council for the emirate of Abu Dhabi would be constituted to assist the ruler. This Executive Council would be "the Government of Abu Dhabi" and would replace the previous Abu Dhabi Council of Ministers (the title of "Minister" is replaced by "Chairman" or "President" of Department and the title "Ministry" by "Department"). The Executive Council would be composed of the "Chairmen of the Departments." According to Article 5 of the Law, 11 departments were to be created, one of which was the Petroleum Department.

This Department was entrusted with all matters relating to petroleum and the petroleum industry in Abu Dhabi, and exercised all the functions of public authority in the field of petroleum under the Abu Dhabi Law on the Conservation of Petroleum Resources. The Department was also charged with the task of defining the oil policy of the emirate, granting exploration permits and oil concessions (after approval by the Executive Council), and fixing the level of oil production (usually in consultation and coordination with ADNOC). The Abu Dhabi Petroleum Department continued to function until the establishment of the Supreme Petroleum Council (SPC) of the emirate of Abu Dhabi in 1988.

The SPC was established by Law No. 1 of 1988 (see Appendix II), and was designed to unify Abu Dhabi's oil planning and supervisory activities. It replaced and assumed all functions of the Petroleum Department and the Board of Directors of ADNOC—the bodies which had previously handled Abu Dhabi's petroleum affairs. The SPC has the authority to control the affairs and establish the policies and objectives of all the sectors of the petroleum industry in Abu Dhabi.

Since its establishment, the SPC has been headed by HH Sheikh Khalifa Bin Zayed Al Nahyan, then Crown Prince of the emirate of Abu Dhabi, and now President of the UAE and Ruler of Abu Dhabi.

3

The Organizational Structure
of the Abu Dhabi Oil Industry

The structure of the Abu Dhabi oil industry is built around the Abu Dhabi National Oil Company (ADNOC). Since its establishment in 1971, ADNOC has assumed the role of a link between government institutions – which establish petroleum policy – and the operating companies that are responsible for executing approved projects. ADNOC is entrusted with the implementation of all aspects of the oil policy of the emirate of Abu Dhabi.

In addition to ADNOC, in the field of exploitation of hydrocarbons, two major operating companies dominated the scene until 1983: the Abu Dhabi Company for Onshore Oil Operations (ADCO) and the Abu Dhabi Marine Operating Company (ADMA-OPCO). ADNOC, through the various participation agreements, holds and manages a 60 percent stake in both of these operating companies on behalf of the government, and exercises a corresponding role in determining their policies and activities. Until the Upper Zakum field (operated by ZADCO) came on stream in 1983, over 90 percent of Abu Dhabi's oil production came from the fields exploited by these two companies. The Abu Dhabi Company for Onshore Oil Operations (ADCO), founded in 1978 as a result of the participation agreements, took over the operations of ADPC. Likewise Abu Dhabi Marine Operating Company (ADMA-OPCO) took over from ADMA in 1977. Currently, the oil industry in Abu Dhabi is dominated by these three major companies: ADCO,

ADMA-OPCO and ZADCO. Besides these, a number of smaller oil companies continue to operate under concession agreements granted in the period 1967–1971. They have been unaffected by the participation arrangements as the government has so far decided not to exercise its options in this respect.

In order to provide a clear picture of the present framework of petroleum activities in Abu Dhabi, this study will focus on ADNOC's establishment, objectives, legal status and relationship with the government. This will be followed by a brief examination of its role, activities and affiliates.

ADNOC: Objectives, Legal Status, Organization and Governmental Relations

ADNOC was established towards the end of 1971 when the wave of "participation" in the producing countries of the region was at its peak. The creation of the government-owned corporation undoubtedly constituted a major step in Abu Dhabi's move to establish control over its oil industry.

The objectives of ADNOC were outlined in Article 3 of the law establishing the company (Law No. 7 of November 27, 1971):

> to work in the oil industry in Abu Dhabi or abroad, and in any stage of the said industry including prospecting and exploration for oil and natural gas and other hydrocarbons, production, refining, transportation and storage of the said materials and any of the by-products thereof. It shall, furthermore, undertake to trade in these materials, by-products and derivatives distribution, sale and exportation [sic].[1]

ADNOC is presently divided into five business directorates that cover its different areas of activity: exploration and production; gas processing; chemicals; refining and marketing; and shared technical services. Each one of these directorates is responsible for overseeing the operations of the ADNOC affiliates carrying out activities in their respective fields. In addition, there are three other directorates with responsibility for administration and management support, finance and human resources.

The Law established ADNOC in the form of a commercial entity: a joint stock company (although the shares are wholly owned by the government) with a separate juridical personality to allow it freedom from administrative constraints and empower it to exercise a reasonable degree of independence in its decision-making and activities. Unlike some national oil companies in the region whose functions include aspects of the state's control of the oil industry (such as the right to grant acreage for exploration and development), ADNOC has no regulatory powers. Control over the oil operating companies (including ADNOC) under Abu Dhabi's Law on the Conservation of Petroleum Resources (1978) was originally exercised by the Department of Petroleum.[2] This Department was replaced in 1988 by the Supreme Petroleum Council (SPC) of Abu Dhabi. The SPC grants prospecting licenses, concessions and petroleum rights and fixes the level of oil production. ADNOC does not define or establish the general oil policy of the state. In fact, it is itself required by Article 19 of its formative law "to adhere to the general oil policy of the state" established by the government.[3]

ADNOC's role as an advisor to the government on oil policy is not stipulated in its statutes, but government decisions on oil policy are, in reality, deeply influenced by ADNOC's analysis and views. Therefore, the company must strike a balance between national interests and the considerations of normal commercial practice.

The initial capital of the company was set at 200 million dirhams (over US$50 million) but in January 1981, ADNOC raised its paid-in capital to 7,500 million dirhams (around $2,000 million).

ADNOC Activities and Achievements

ADNOC's activities today are vast and diverse. They cover almost all phases of the petroleum industry, including oil and gas exploration, development, production, processing and refining, local distribution of refined products, marketing of oil and gas abroad, marine transportation, and intensive involvement in the field of petroleum services and industrial projects based on oil and gas.

First and foremost among ADNOC's activities today is its involvement in the production of oil and gas, which can be considered the cornerstone of its overall operation. Since the early stages of its operation ADNOC has been aware of the importance of having its own source of crude oil and gas in order to integrate its operations. Indeed, an oil company cannot safely embark on the vast and multiple operations required by the oil industry without basing these operations on a secure supply of oil and gas. ADNOC therefore focused on solidifying its control over oil production operations.

ADNOC also realized that in addition to oil and gas production, it would need to carry out other complementary activities stemming from a number of considerations, most of which are common to national oil companies in the producing countries of the third world. It had to:

- conduct a fully integrated operation covering the largest possible range of functions, activities and basic services of the oil industry in order to avoid being absent or excluded from any important sector of the oil business;
- contribute to the industrialization of Abu Dhabi in compliance with the policy of industrialization based on oil and gas – being the main natural resources – and in pursuance of the aim embodied in its charter that calls for the maximum utilization of petroleum resources for the benefit of the national economy;

- secure more fruitful investment of oil revenues and diversify income sources (avoiding complete dependence, as in the past, on income derived from crude oil sales);
- provide functions such as petroleum services, especially those presenting a certain degree of strategic importance to the industry; and
- provide a large number of nationals with the opportunity to gain technical and managerial experience and practical training in the oil industry.

ADNOC decided to undertake some of these activities independently, while others could be accomplished through cooperation or joint ventures with foreign partners.

Exploration and Production

As mentioned earlier, the creation of ADNOC in 1971 coincided with the peak of the trend in the oil-producing countries for national participation in existing concessions. However, it was not until the General Agreement on Participation was concluded in late 1972 – which came into effect on January 1, 1973 – that the government of Abu Dhabi (and through it, ADNOC) acquired a 25 percent stake in the two major concessionary companies in its territory—ADPC for onshore operations and ADMA for offshore operations.

ADNOC also became involved in the field of exploration and production through: (1) the separate arrangements initiated by ADNOC to exploit certain oil fields outside the scope of the major concessions; (2) the promulgation of Law No. 4 of 1976 on Abu Dhabi's ownership of all associated and non-associated gas; and (3) the decision of the government in 1979 to grant ADNOC prospecting licenses.

Participation Agreements and the Roles of ADNOC and the Operating Companies:

The participation agreements of 1974 were concluded between the four principal oil producers of the region (Saudi Arabia, Kuwait, Qatar and Abu Dhabi) and the major international oil companies. These participation arrangements were nullified in Saudi Arabia, Kuwait and Qatar as a result of complete takeovers of the major operating companies by their respective governments. As Abu Dhabi retains these participation arrangements as a framework for its relationships with foreign oil companies, it therefore provides an interesting model for successful participatory arrangements.

Abu Dhabi concluded two participation agreements in 1974—one with ADMA and the other with ADCO. The agreements were brief and contained general principles stipulating that an implementation agreement was to be concluded to provide detailed arrangements and procedures. The main provisions of the preliminary ADMA agreement can be summarized as follows:

- ADNOC and ADMA were each entitled to lift – in each quarter – their share of the crude oil available (i.e., 60 percent for ADNOC and 40 percent for the ADMA shareholders).
- The parties were to establish a Joint Management Committee (JMC) composed of their representatives. In the case of ADMA, the JMC consists of six members of whom two are appointed by the government (representing ADNOC). The JMC is responsible for all major policy matters relating to management (including exploration, development and work programs, capital and operating expenditures, and the appointment and removal of key personnel). ADNOC holds 60 percent of the votes and ADMA the remaining 40 percent, but decisions of the JMC require 75 percent of the vote. In order to offset the effects of this high majority requirement, a sole risk clause stipulates that "in the

event that the requisite majority is not obtained in favour of any capital expenditure project, the government may nevertheless go ahead with such project and shall put up the whole of the related expenditures and enjoy the whole of the related benefits." [4]

- Operations are conducted on behalf of the parties by an operating company incorporated in Abu Dhabi under Abu Dhabi law. Of its capital, 60 percent is held by ADNOC and 40 percent by ADMA.

This new agreement improved upon those before it by immediately giving the host country the majority of the equity in the venture, which granted the national company a preponderant role in the management and running of operations—although the 75 percent majority required for passing important decisions by the JMC provides an effective veto to the foreign partners.

A sound assessment of this agreement should not, however, be based solely on the provisions it contains, but on the manner in which participation is effectively implemented and more specifically on: (1) the manner in which the national company exercises its right to market its equity share; and (2) the contents of the implementing agreement and the status and functioning of the operating company created.

Abu Dhabi provides an interesting model of a successful implementing agreement concluded within the framework of a participation agreement. The preparation and negotiation of the required implementing agreements with ADPC and ADMA took much longer than expected. The agreement concluded with ADCO took four years to be finalized and was not signed until September 1978; the agreement with ADMA was concluded in April 1977. The main provisions of the implementing agreement with ADMA, which are still in effect, are as follows:

- Operations are conducted on behalf of the parties by a non-profit operating company (called ADMA-OPCO) incorporated in Abu Dhabi and governed by the laws of the emirate. The principal office of the company is in Abu Dhabi, therefore ADMA, as interim operator, undertook to transfer to Abu Dhabi all documents, accounting records and papers pertaining to operations in Abu Dhabi (previously kept in London from where operations were directed). Sixty percent of the capital of ADMA-OPCO is held by ADNOC and 40 percent by the ADMA shareholders.

- ADMA-OPCO has a Board of Directors to manage its affairs, composed of five members—two nominated by ADNOC and one nominated by each of the three shareholders in ADMA. The Chairman of the Board and the General Manager of the Company are chosen from among ADNOC's candidates. According to Article VI(a) of the Articles of Association of ADMA-OPCO, the resolutions of the Board relating to routine management issues are taken by a simple majority of three, which must include the two members from ADNOC. By contrast, matters of policy come within the jurisdiction of the JMC as described above and thus require a 75 percent majority.

- In selecting contractors, preference is given to national contractors and contracting companies, provided they are technically qualified and their prices do not exceed their competitors' prices by more than 10 percent; a similar priority is given to national retailers when purchasing goods and materials.

- The company undertakes to follow an active policy of hiring personnel in order to ensure the development of its own staff (instead of almost complete reliance on the secondees of one of the partners, as was once the case). When recruiting, the company must abide by the government's policy of

Arabization,[5] and for this purpose it conducts appropriate training schemes.

- Each party has the right to receive a proportionate share in production. Each party is responsible for the payment of the applicable income tax and royalty on its share. In accordance with the OPEC Formula, the rate of income tax applicable is 85 percent and the royalty is 20 percent to be expensed (i.e., to be considered as one of the expenditures of the chargeable party and to be deducted from its gross revenue to determine its net income).

- The agreement also regulates the technical assistance provided by the parties to the operating company—to avoid instances, as in the past, when almost all the secondees come from one shareholder. It also provides for the creation of advisory committees and for the procedures and schedules for the preparation of operating and capital budgets. The agreement is governed by Abu Dhabi law and disputes are settled by arbitration in Abu Dhabi in accordance with International Chamber of Commerce (ICC) rules and regulations. An annex containing detailed accounting and financial procedures is attached to prevent ambiguities and disputes.

- Another feature of the implementing agreement is the establishment of different advisory committees to the Board, composed of the representatives of the participants. Initially, four such committees were established: the Technical Committee; the Finance Committee; the Contracts and Projects Committee; and the Supply Coordination Committee.

ADNOC is involved in the operations of ADMA-OPCO through:

- its Arab secondees and employees who are working in the company alongside non-Arab foreign secondees and employees, thus enabling Arab staff to gain direct experience through their daily involvement;

- its representatives on the different advisory committees who discuss with the representatives of the other parties all technical, financial and other problems for the purpose of making recommendations to the Board;
- its representatives on the Board of Directors of the OPCO; and
- its representatives on the JMC which decides major policy matters.

The experience gained and results achieved depend more on the manner in which the national partner accomplishes its tasks at these different levels than on an abstract interpretation of the text of the agreement. So it is really up to ADNOC to protect Abu Dhabi's interests.

Participation should not be a "nominal contribution," but an actual and effective contribution by all participants. The participation arrangement has achieved positive results for Abu Dhabi, the most important of which has been the exploitation of oil and gas in strict accordance with the potential of the fields and in conformity with its interests. In past years, ADNOC has concentrated on improving the expertise of its technical staff in the fields of geology and reservoir engineering in order to prepare technical studies and to make adequate plans. After long discussions with its partners, ADNOC has been able to convince them to agree to its plans and to the allocation of the required funds.

Concerning the benefits derived from partnerships and joint ventures, it is clear that dialogue with international partners is of great value in final decision-making. Furthermore, participation has opened the door to ADNOC staff, allowing them to be involved in production operations and oil field development.

Therefore, the implementing agreements discussed above have been satisfactory to all parties concerned and have been realized without any serious difficulties. The government of Abu Dhabi feels that through these agreements and arrangements it has accomplished its basic objectives: effective control of the production phase of the industry;[6] real participation in the decision-making process; and gaining experience and training for its nationals while securing the contribution of knowledge and expertise from foreign partners. This is why, at present, Abu Dhabi's government appears to be content with the 60 percent participation arrangement and has not been inclined to follow the trend of taking over major operating companies in their entirety, as in Kuwait, Qatar and Saudi Arabia.

Developments beyond the Scope of the Major Concessions:

ADNOC's role in exploration and production also involves the development of certain oil fields separately, outside the scope of the operations of the major operating companies. The fields earmarked for development under this arrangement are all offshore and were originally discovered by ADMA and included in its concession. The need for ADNOC's involvement arose as a result of the initial reluctance of the foreign partners in ADMA to join these ventures on an equity basis—they delayed development on the grounds that the returns under the participation arrangements were insufficient to meet the relatively high investment required to develop these offshore fields. JODCO agreed to join ADNOC in these ventures (retaining an equity share of 12 percent in some). The arrangements concluded that cover these three fields are as follows:

- **Upper Zakum Field and the Formation of ZADCO**
  An operating company, ZADCO, was created in 1977 to handle the development of this field. The operating company is equally owned by ADNOC and Total (CFP at the time of ZADCO's

creation). However, the 50–50 ratio applies only to operational decisions since Total does not have an equity share in the field. ADNOC initially retained an 88 percent equity interest in the venture while JODCO held – and continues to hold – 12 percent, receiving a similar proportion of crude production as equity oil and contributing the same percentage of required investment. (In early 2005, ADNOC agreed to sell 28 percent of its equity interest in this field to the US group ExxonMobil. ADNOC's interest was thus reduced to 60 percent, while JODCO retained its 12 percent.)

- **Umm Al Dalkh Field and the Creation of UDECO**
  The agreement for the development of Umm Al-Dalkh field was finalized in September 1978. As part of the agreement, ADNOC and JODCO established a 50–50 joint operating company – Umm Al-Dalkh Development Company (UDECO) – to handle management and operational decisions. JODCO, which holds a 12 percent equity stake in the venture, has the right to lift 12 percent of crude production as equity oil and a further 20 percent for a determined period at ADNOC's standard price, terms and conditions for crude oil sales.

- **Dalma, Satah and Jarnain Fields**
  An agreement was reached in July 1990 between ADNOC and JODCO for the development of these three offshore fields which were previously included in the ADMA concession.

ADNOC's Prospecting Licenses:

In April 1980 the Executive Council of Abu Dhabi granted ADNOC exclusive rights to the exploration and development of hydrocarbons in five blocks (two onshore and three offshore) within exploratory areas that were not covered by any existing petroleum agreements. In these areas ADNOC has the right to carry out all the operations and activities contained in its establishing law. The decision of 1980 constituted a major step forward in the state's efforts to ensure more control over its national oil industry, and was undoubtedly an important milestone in ADNOC's development. It provided the national company with the opportunity to strengthen its grip on Abu Dhabi's oil industry, consolidate its operations and gain invaluable first-hand experience of exploration and production operations. The resultant exploration program adopted by ADNOC led to a substantial increase in proven oil and gas reserves in the country.

Exploration and Production Operations

As mentioned earlier, three major operating companies – ADCO (onshore), ADMA-OPCO and ZADCO (both offshore) – dominate the oil scene in Abu Dhabi. These three companies are responsible for all exploration, development and production operations in their respective concession areas and account for almost all of Abu Dhabi's output of oil and gas.[7]

In view of Abu Dhabi's huge reserves, the exploration programs of the operating companies essentially aim to acquire more accurate data about known reserves and structures rather than make fresh discoveries. However, through the execution of these programs, the operating companies have on occasion located additional reserves.

In 2005 Abu Dhabi's total oil production was about 2,250,000 bpd of which ADCO (onshore) produced around 1,230,000 bpd, ADMA and ZADCO (both offshore) produced around 960,000 bpd (560,000 bpd for ADMA and 400,000 bpd for ZADCO), and the other four small companies accounted for 60,000 bpd between them.[8]

Abu Dhabi has maintained its efforts to step up its production capacity. It was reported in 2004 that the emirate had a spare capacity of at least 500,000 bpd, but that the authorities had set a target for the operating companies to increase total production capacity to around 3 mbpd by 2006 and 3.7 mbpd by 2010. As of yet, there are no reports to confirm that the target figure for 2006 was achieved.

ADNOC's Independent Activities

Marketing

ADNOC quickly realized that reliance on foreign oil companies to market its own share of oil would keep it in a weak position. The company was also aware of the importance of retaining direct independent contacts with international markets, thereby establishing relationships while building its reputation and experience.

ADNOC's first experience in this field came in 1973 after the conclusion of the first participation agreement, when it sold its share of equity oil (amounting to 32,000 bpd) to the Japanese company Japan Line. ADNOC's direct sales went on to increase dramatically, while the company continued to implement its policy of expanding its markets and diversifying its clients.

Some of the core principles of ADNOC's marketing policy have been to avoid dealing with intermediaries; to severely restrict the resale of its crude; and not to participate in spot market sales. Most of its clients have been independent, medium sized oil companies (although some Majors are among its clients) which possess refineries and outlets of their own. A small number of government to government sales contracts have been signed but they cover limited quantities and have been of marginal significance in terms of ADNOC's overall marketing operation. ADNOC currently markets its entire share of oil and gas as well as refined products.

Refining

Refining activity is an important link in the chain of operations of an integrated oil industry and all major oil companies have their own refining capability. The economic advantages for a producing country of refining part of its oil production rather than exporting all of its crude are well known: it contributes to the accelerated economic development and industrialization of the country; provides advanced skills and technical experience; and allows the country to receive the optimum value of its natural resources. This is the reasoning behind the prevailing trend among OPEC and OAPEC members to complain about their minimal share of the world's refining capacity. For ADNOC, an additional factor that adds to the importance of possessing a refining capacity is its obligation to satisfy the demands of local consumption.

Abu Dhabi currently has two wholly-owned refineries: a small plant at Umm Al Nar with a capacity of 88,000 bpd which was opened in 1976; and another at Ruwais with a capacity of 420,000 bpd which was established in 1982 and intended to be export-oriented. In 1999, a company owned by ADNOC – Abu Dhabi Oil Refining Company (TAKREER) – was established to take over responsibility for refining operations and to develop the refining industry. Takreer is presently installing unleaded gasoline units at both its refineries, as well as a low-sulfur gas oil unit.

Local Distribution of Refined Products

As early as 1973, the government decided that the local distribution of refined products should be carried out by a national entity instead of foreign oil distribution companies. For that purpose ADNOC Distribution, a company owned by ADNOC, was established in 1973 (by Law No. 13 of 1973). This company handles all domestic marketing activities, takes delivery of products supplied by local refineries and undertakes their distribution throughout the emirate, also securing the importation of additional quantities to meet any deficit. ADNOC Distribution operates a vast network of service stations throughout the emirate of Abu Dhabi.

Furthermore, the ADNOC Aviation Refueling Service began operations in 1982 at Abu Dhabi International Airport and the company now refuels more than 50 international airlines. A lubricant blending and packaging plant, commissioned by the company in 1979, has developed and expanded to become what ADNOC describes as "one of the best plants in the region."[9] The company has also invested extensively in state-of-the-art bunkering facilities at the Mina Zayed Port in Abu Dhabi—one of its functions is to refuel ships.[10]

ADNOC Distribution is now installing a natural gas distribution network in the emirate, which will have the effect of broadening the utilization of gas as a domestic energy source. This network will deliver gas to around 200,000 industrial users and households in the cities of Abu Dhabi and Al Ain and in the Mussafah industrial zone. The initial phase of this project is scheduled for completion in 2008.[11]

Marine Transportation

In order to secure effective participation in the field of marine transportation to complement its marketing activity abroad, ADNOC established a wholly-owned subsidiary – the Abu Dhabi National Tankers Company (ADNATCO) – in 1975 to engage in all marine operations involving the transportation of crude oil, natural gas, refined petroleum products and all other hydrocarbon-based substances.

ADNATCO owns and operates a fleet of nine tankers, including a molten sulfur carrier, a bunkering vessel, and roll-on roll-off (ro-ro) vessels. ADNATCO vessels deliver worldwide to customers including major oil companies, and provide logistical support and advice on shipping to ADNOC and its group of companies. In addition to managing and operating its own fleet, ADNATCO manages ADNOC's offshore bunker supply ships.[12]

National Drilling Company (NDC)

The National Drilling Company (NDC) was established in May 1972 to handle drilling operations required for exploration and field development as well as to undertake work and maintenance operations in both onshore and offshore areas.

Today, NDC is a leading drilling company and one of the largest drilling contractors in the Middle East, currently operating a modern fleet of ten offshore and twelve onshore drilling rigs. In addition, NDC has six water well rigs surveying ground water in Abu Dhabi and Al Ain. The company has won a number of awards for health and safety standards, and for its innovative approach.[13]

Ruwais Industrial Zone: Infrastructure and Utilities

In order to achieve its objective of industrialization based on oil and gas, ADNOC decided to establish a petroleum industrial complex at Ruwais, near Jebel Dhanna which is considered the most appropriate port for exporting oil and gas products from onshore oil fields in Abu Dhabi.

The facilities available at the Ruwais Industrial Zone include jetties, berths, stores, warehouses, roads, camps, workshops, a telecommunications system, water and sewage systems and other temporary and permanent utilities. ADNOC has also established power facilities and desalination plants for various uses. A housing complex has been constructed to accommodate employees working on various projects in the Ruwais area.

The Ruwais area has been transformed from bare desert into Abu Dhabi's biggest industrial zone—a cornerstone of its economic development. Some of the industrial projects there are carried out by ADNOC (such as the refinery referred to above), and others through joint ventures between ADNOC and foreign partners.

Activities through Joint Ventures with Foreign Partners

Other ADNOC activities are executed and performed in cooperation with foreign partners. It was thought that through partnerships with specialized foreign companies, ADNOC would benefit from: advanced managerial and technological expertise; marketing knowledge and outlets (when needed); and the opportunity for the company's staff and employees to gain direct experience through working with the experienced personnel of a foreign partner.

In light of these considerations, and the power granted to ADNOC by its statutes to "establish companies, independently or in association with others, or participate in companies already in existence,"[14] ADNOC approached a number of highly specialized foreign companies in a variety of fields for the purpose of concluding appropriate joint venture arrangements.

A number of these joint ventures were concluded involving well-known companies including Shell (in GASCO), BP (in ADGAS), Total (in GASCO, ADGAS and the Ruwais Fertilizer Project—FERTIL) and Mitsui (in ADGAS) in the field of gas projects. In the field of petroleum services they include Consolidated Construction Company (in the National Petroleum Construction Company—NPCC); N.L. Industries (in Abu Dhabi Drilling Chemicals and Products – ADDCAP – which has been recently merged with ADNOC's wholly owned subsidiary, Esnaad); and more recently Borealis A/S (in Abu Dhabi Polymers Company Ltd.—Borouge).

In order for these joint ventures to achieve the basic objectives assigned to them, ADNOC adopted a legal framework incorporating certain standard clauses and provisions.

These clauses and provisions dictate that a foreign company shares the total investment required for the project and provides a part of the share capital of the joint company. The foreign company therefore becomes a full partner, deeply involved in the life of the project and thus committed to its success. However, ADNOC always retains the majority of the equity in order to be able to play a major role in the decision-making process, defining the policy of the project and establishing its plans and work programs to safeguard national interests. ADNOC's share is never less than 51 percent. In the majority of cases its share is 60 percent, and in some cases it is even more: 66.7 percent in FERTIL, 68 percent in GASCO and 75 percent in NPCC.

For the implementation and operation of projects, the parties jointly establish a limited liability company in Abu Dhabi in accordance with the laws of the country. Since establishing companies and corporations in Abu Dhabi requires governmental authorization, these companies are established by a decree. The headquarters of the joint companies are situated in Abu Dhabi, as are their records and accounts (unlike the old concessionary companies which used to run their operations from headquarters located abroad).

The fully paid-up share capital of the joint companies represent between 20 and 25 percent of the total financial requirements of the project. ADNOC and the foreign partner subscribe to the share capital on a pro rata basis. To provide the balance of the total funds needed, the parties seek loans and provide guarantees corresponding to their shareholdings in the joint company. Sometimes the loan is provided by an Abu Dhabi governmental financial agency, such as the Abu Dhabi Investment Authority (ADIA), in which case ADNOC and the foreign partners provide guarantees proportionately. In other cases the loan is secured through a consortium of banks, often led by the National Bank of Abu Dhabi (NBAD).

The initial life of the company varies between seven and ten years for those dealing in petroleum services (renewable for a short period or periods, of two years each) thus allowing ADNOC to become the sole shareholder in a relatively short period should it choose to. For industrial projects, their nature warrants a longer period varying from 25 to 30 years.

In terms of management and administration, the business of the company is managed by a Board of Directors composed of a number of shareholders' representatives (in proportion to their respective shareholding interests and resulting in an ADNOC majority). The Chairman of the Board is appointed from among ADNOC's directors. Resolutions of the board are passed by a simple majority provided it comprises at least one Director appointed by the foreign partner. Certain important decisions require unanimous approval of the shareholders (e.g., alteration of articles of association or the share capital).

The affairs of the company are directed by a General Manager (GM) and a Deputy General Manager (DGM). For the initial three to four years after the establishment of the company, the GM is appointed by the foreign partner and the DGM by ADNOC. Thereafter, ADNOC nominates the GM and the foreign partner nominates the DGM.

A standard clause states that the company shall pursue an active policy of developing its own staff and resources to achieve "self sufficiency" in the shortest possible time, giving recruitment priority to qualified nationals and adopting training schemes for their advancement. However, the foreign partner undertakes to make available to the joint company the necessary technology, know-how and expertise, and to provide it, at preferential rates (or at cost), with technical assistance (including secondment of personnel) to enable it to carry out work efficiently and economically.

In terms of the marketing of products, one of two alternative arrangements is adopted: either the joint company does all the marketing on behalf of the shareholders (this is the case for ADGAS and FERTIL) or each shareholder takes its share of the products and markets that share individually (as in the case of GASCO).

In principle, the new company and its shareholders are subject to the laws of Abu Dhabi including those pertaining to taxation and duties. Presently, activities in the field of petroleum services are not taxed (unlike the activities of oil-producing companies). For the industrial projects based on gas (e.g., ADGAS, GASCO and FERTIL) a special fiscal regime has been adopted which is much more favorable to them than the general system applicable to oil companies in order to encourage the exploitation of natural gas resources, attract the heavy investment required and take into account the particular hazards of this field (see Chapter 4).

The agreement between ADNOC and the foreign partner is construed and governed in accordance with the laws of Abu Dhabi (and the UAE). The company itself is subject to all such laws and regulations. In the event of a dispute arising under the agreements, the matter is settled through arbitration held in Abu Dhabi under the Rules of Conciliation and Arbitration of the ICC. This legal structure of the joint ventures has proven successful in ensuring harmonious relations between the parties and the smooth running of the enterprises involved. The joint ventures concluded by ADNOC can be classified as belonging to one of two main categories: industrial projects and petroleum services organizations.

Industrial Projects

Foremost among these joint ventures are the industrial projects based on gas and petrochemicals. They include ADGAS, which handles the liquefaction of offshore gas (ADNOC initially retained a 51 percent equity interest in ADGAS that grew to 70 percent in 1997), and GASCO, for the exploitation of onshore associated gas, in which ADNOC holds a 68 percent equity interest.[15] The industrial projects also include two companies in the field of petrochemicals—FERTIL and Borouge:

- **Ruwais Fertilizer Industries (FERTIL)**
  FERTIL was established in 1980 as a joint venture between ADNOC and CFP (now Total—two-thirds and one-third ownership respectively). This company was established to produce ammonia and urea using associated gas from onshore fields or the tail (residual) gas resulting from the extraction of natural gas liquids (NGLs) at the GASCO NGL extraction plants located within the onshore fields. The complex, located in the Ruwais Industrial Zone, consists of ammonia and urea processing plants. The installed capacity of the ammonia plant is 1,050 metric tons per day and for the urea plant is 1,500 metric tons per day. Fifteen percent of the annual production is marketed locally in the UAE and 85 percent in external markets.

- **Abu Dhabi Polymers Company Limited (Borouge)**
  Established in 1998, Borouge is a synergistic joint venture between ADNOC and one of Europe's leading polyolefins producers, Borealis A/S, that manufactures and sells polyethylene for use in technically demanding applications—primarily in the flexible and rigid packaging and construction industries. The complex produces 450,000 tons of high and linear low-density polyethylene per year.[16]

Petroleum Services Organizations

ADNOC is also involved in petroleum services, which are indispensable for providing technical support for the basic activities related to the production of oil and gas. The company's effective participation in this sector, aside from allowing it to perform a strategic function that is intimately linked with basic oil activity, provides it with an opportunity to gain advanced technological knowledge. ADNOC has contracted highly specialized companies with extensive experience in different fields within the petroleum industry and established joint companies with them in which it retains at least 51 percent of their equity. These petroleum services companies include NPCC, with a 70 percent share held by ADNOC; National Marine Services (NMS), initially with a 60 percent share held ADNOC (now replaced by the wholly owned subsidiary Esnaad);[17] and Abu Dhabi Petroleum Ports Operating Company (ADPPOC), renamed IRSHAD in 2002 and now wholly owned by ADNOC.

The NPCC is a joint venture between ADNOC (70 percent) and CCC (30 percent). It was established in 1973 and began operations in 1974. Today, NPCC offers comprehensive services as a major engineering, procurement and construction contractor for both the onshore and offshore oil, gas and petrochemicals industry. Services provided by NPCC include the construction of steel structures, pressure vessels, storage tanks and spheres and anti-corrosion coating of pipes. The NPCC also operates a marine fleet for offshore transportation and the installation of structures and submarine pipe laying.[18]

Overall, ADNOC occupies a prime position in the basic phase of the oil industry (production) in terms of the quantity of oil at its disposal (all of which is marketed directly), its percentage of total production, and the effective role it plays in the monitoring of oil production and the industry's decision-making process. It has a significant presence in most stages of the integrated oil business, including refining, local distribution, marine transportation, and processing and liquefaction of gas. ADNOC has assembled a broad collection of affiliates and subsidiaries covering a wide array of petroleum services, has put an end to the flaring of associated natural gas and has established a large industrial zone with a variety of gas-based industries.

4

Abu Dhabi's Gas Experience

Owing to the growing importance of gas as a source of energy, natural gas production and processing facilities continue to expand rapidly in Abu Dhabi. The emirate already possesses one of the world's largest non-associated gas reservoirs in the Khuff formation beneath the Umm Shaif oil field. In addition, onshore and offshore associated and non-associated gas fields are being developed to meet rising domestic demand and provide feedstock for export projects.

Major programs are currently being implemented in Abu Dhabi to expand gas recovery, processing, liquefaction and export capacities. Furthermore, a number of new discoveries have been made in recent years of both associated and non-associated gas, boosting the emirate's reserves substantially.

The most important element in the legal framework of the gas industry in Abu Dhabi is law No. 4 of 1976, which established the government's sole ownership over associated and non-associated gas resources located in the emirate. These resources initially came under the old-style concession agreements. As a result, the flaring of associated gas by oil companies in the Middle East was, for a long period, one of the main complaints of the host countries and a source of constant friction between them and the oil companies.

According to Law No. 4, the government (represented by ADNOC) has complete control over the exploitation of gas in the emirate. Oil companies must relinquish all gas discovered to the government (except for the associated gas required for their operations). One of the legal consequences of this law is that ADNOC is the sole supplier of gas feedstock for gas projects in Abu Dhabi.

This chapter is divided into three sections. The first will deal with development and production operations; the second with gas processing operations; and the third with the marketing of liquefied natural gas (LNG) and liquefied petroleum gas (LPG) contracts.

Development and Production Operations

ADNOC's policy in the field of gas development is geared towards meeting local energy and industrial requirements, producing LNG and LPG for export, and preventing gas wastage through flaring. ADNOC's first priority in this regard was the gathering and utilization of associated gases produced with crude oil from the different onshore and offshore oil fields—where gas was being flared in the late 1970s. To this end, a number of gas treatment and processing plants were installed both onshore and offshore, supported by gas gathering systems and pipeline networks to ensure maximum recovery of gas produced (further gas gathering and treatment projects are also currently under construction). ADNOC's attention then turned to developing natural gas reservoirs to ensure a stable supply of gas to local users and to export projects. Associated gas from the onshore fields is now fed into the emirate's extensive gas gathering system for supply to fractionating plants, while dry gas is consumed directly by power stations, desalination plants and the fertilizer complex at Ruwais.[1]

Onshore facilities for recycling gas from GASCO back to ADCO were completed in 1985, when the project for injecting gas into the Thamama C reservoir at Habshan was approved. The aim of this project is to utilize the surplus gas from the Thamama C plant, injecting it into the reservoir to raise the pressure and aid recovery.

Offshore, the Umm Shaif gas development program was completed in 1988, consisting of two wellhead platforms with a capacity of 150 million cubic feet per day (cfpd) each, and two injector/producer platforms, all of which are connected to the Umm Shaif "Supercomplex." Part of the gas produced is re-injected into the Uweinat reservoir to maintain its pressure, but it can be diverted to the main processing plant in the event of a shortfall.

A current priority is to develop non-associated gas production from both onshore and offshore structures. Onshore, plans have been made to increase the output of associated and non-associated gas from the Bab and Asab fields through two major gas development projects (AGD-2 and AGD-3) which are intended to boost gas production by around 2 billion cfpd in 2007, while offshore gas production has been increased by the development of the Khuff gas structure discovered under the Abu Al-Bukhoosh oil field, 45 km northeast of Das Island.

Offshore gas production has also risen as a result of further development work at the Umm Shaif field, where production capacity was increased to provide the additional feedstock needed for the expanded Das Island LNG plant. Discoveries of Khuff gas reservoirs and other non-associated gas structures, together with the expansion of associated gas recovery systems, have boosted the emirate's gas reserves substantially in recent years. While Abu Dhabi's proven gas reserves were estimated at 188.4 billion cubic feet on January 1, 1995, at the beginning of 2005 they were estimated at 198.5 billion cubic feet.[2]

The emirate has also successfully stepped up its gross gas production; while production was running at around 2.45 billion cfpd at the beginning of 1995, it was raised to around 6.8 billion cfpd in 2005.[3] The aim of Abu Dhabi's rapid development of its gas reserves is to provide additional gas for export and to meet the requirements of the domestic market in the emirate of Abu Dhabi and the wider UAE. Thus, gas consumption will continue to grow rapidly. The gas network currently being installed by ADNOC Distribution in Abu Dhabi and Al Ain will lead to a broadening of the utilization of natural gas as a domestic energy source and will require additional quantities of gas. This growing consumption of gas was one of the incentives for Abu Dhabi's promotion of the Dolphin Project. Within the framework of this project, Abu Dhabi planned to start importing natural gas from Qatar in 2006.[4]

The Dolphin Project[5]

The Dolphin Project is an ambitious project which was promoted by the Abu Dhabi government's wholly owned UAE Offset Group (UOG), launched in 1998. The project aims to establish a supply of up to two billion cfpd of Qatari natural gas, piped through a 350 km subsea gas line to Taweelah in Abu Dhabi and Jebel Ali in Dubai. The project is being implemented by UOG in conjunction with two international oil companies—Total and Occidental Petroleum. A 25-year project development agreement was signed between the parties in March 2000, providing for the establishment of a joint venture company, Dolphin Energy Ltd. (DEL) in which UOG holds a 51 percent interest and its partners 24.5 percent each.

The agreement calls for an 800 km gas line (of which 350 km is subsea) to be built to carry Qatari gas from the North Field to Abu Dhabi and Dubai in the first instance, and later to Oman and possibly Pakistan. In September 2005 Dolphin and Oman Oil Company (OOC) announced an agreement regarding the future supply of Dolphin gas to Oman, to assist the Sultanate's own industrialization plan in the northwest.[6] The pipeline will have a capacity of 57 million cubic meters per day of gas. A sales and purchase agreement was signed in 2002 between the Qatari government and DEL for the export of 57 million cubic meters per day of gas to the UAE. The total investment in the project is estimated at some US$8–10 billion. The cost of the first phase of the project is estimated at $3.5 billion ($2 billion for the upstream facilities, and $1.5 billion for the gas line and terminals in Abu Dhabi and Dubai).

At the end of 2003, Qatar Petroleum and DEL finalized the Dolphin Project's field development plan in accordance with a 25-year development and production-sharing agreement reached in December 2001. When the development plan has been completed (due in 2007), DEL will produce natural gas from the North Field and process it in an offshore plant at Ras Laffan (in Qatar) where condensate and NGL will be extracted. Gas will then be transported through the Dolphin gas line.

During the implementation of the Dolphin Project, DEL began concluding gas supply agreements with future buyers of Qatari gas. In October 2003, a 25-year agreement was signed between DEL and the Abu Dhabi Water and Electricity Authority (ADWEA), committing DEL to supply the necessary quantities of Dolphin gas to four affiliates of ADWEA. A similar agreement was signed between DEL and Union Water and Electricity Co., another company controlled by the emirate of Abu Dhabi.

Gas Processing Operations

Besides the processing plants owned and operated by ADNOC for domestic use (e.g., the two natural gas processing plants Thamama F and Thamama C, both in the Habshan area of the Bab field), ADNOC entered into two joint ventures with foreign partners to establish major companies in the field of gas processing: ADGAS and GASCO.

Abu Dhabi Gas Liquefaction Company (ADGAS)[7]

ADGAS processes and exports LNG, LPG and Pentane Plus from its plant on Das Island, situated 160 km northwest of Abu Dhabi city. Since the plant commenced operations in 1977 the LNG and LPG have been delivered to the Tokyo Electric Power Company Inc. (TEPCO). When it came on stream in 1977, it was the most complex LNG plant in the world, with 11 gas systems incorporating a wide range of pressures and compositions. It consists of two identical process trains in parallel, arranged to permit safe plant overhaul of one train while the other remains in service. The two liquefaction trains were initially designed to produce a total annual yield of 2,230,000 tons of LNG; 650,000 tons of Propane; 420,000 tons of Butane; and 320,000 tons of Pentane Plus.

Management and Administration of ADGAS

The law establishing ADGAS stipulated that the company should operate pursuant to the articles of association issued by the shareholders and that the articles should specify voting rights and the method of appointing the Board of Directors. The Chairman of the Board of Directors is appointed by the Board from among the candidates nominated by ADNOC; the Vice-Chairman is designated by the Board from those nominated by the other shareholders (excluding ADNOC). The decisions of the Board of Directors are adopted by the votes of a Director or Directors nominated by ADNOC and present at the meeting and the votes of a Director elected by one of the other shareholders. However, some matters – usually those of particular importance – require the votes of the Director or Directors nominated by ADNOC and present at the meeting, the vote of a Director nominated by a holder of "class B" shares (shares held by BP or Total) and that of a Director nominated by a holder of "class C" shares (shares held by Mitsui Group). Such matters include, *inter alia*:

- the amendment of articles of association;
- any reduction or increase in the share capital of the company;
- terms for acquisition of borrowed funds;
- capital expenditure in excess of a certain amount; and
- the appointment of the General Manager.

Gas Availability, Supply and Gathering Facilities

ADGAS receives associated gas primarily from the offshore oil fields of Umm Shaif and Zakum. The quantity of gas received depends upon the crude oil production levels of these fields. Gas from the Uweinat gas cap supplements this associated gas supply.

The gas gathering facilities for delivery of gas to the plant are operated on behalf of ADNOC by ADMA-OPCO. ADMA-OPCO is owned by ADNOC (60 percent), BP (14⅔ percent), CFP (13⅓ percent) and JODCO (12 percent).

The original gas gathering facilities were constructed by ADMA, and additional gas gathering facilities have been constructed since the plant was commissioned and are owned by ADNOC.

ADGAS makes payments to ADNOC and to ADMA-OPCO for the operation and use of the gas gathering facilities. In addition, ADGAS pays ADNOC for the supply of gas feedstock for the LNG plant.

Shareholders' Support

ADGAS is self-sufficient with respect to the conduct of its normal operations. There are separate technical service agreements with each of the four shareholders (ADNOC, BP, CFP and Mitsui) under which ADGAS can call for specialist technical advice and assistance. For major technical assistance ADGAS may either call on its shareholders or look to appropriate third party specialists and/or contractors.

Expansion Project (3rd LNG Train)

Expansion Project (3rd LNG Train)

ADGAS completed a major project to double the capacity of the Das Island plant through the addition of a third gas train which has a capacity of 2.3 million tons per year of LNG and 250,000 tons per year of LPG. Feedstock for the new train consists of both associated gas from the Umm Shaif and Zakum fields and non-associated gas from the Umm Shaif and Abu Al-Bukhoosh fields. Additional gas is lifted for TEPCO over a 25-year period, pursuant to the sales purchase agreement between ADGAS and TEPCO (signed on October 3, 1993) which provided for an increase in its purchases to 4.3 million tons per year of LNG and 750,000 tons per year of LPG with effect from 1994. In addition to its term contracts, ADGAS began selling LNG on the spot market in the late 1990s.

Transportation of Exported Gas

Initially, shipping capacity had been arranged pursuant to two contracts of affreightment (COAs) between ADGAS and the Liquefied Gas Shipping Company (LGSC). LGSC was a company with identical ownership to that of ADGAS and was registered in Bermuda. Each COA bound LGSC to load and transport LNG and LPG from Das Island to TEPCO in Tokyo Bay. Under each COA, ADGAS was obliged to pay the total freight costs incurred by LGSC and – in respect of LNG – an additional amount in the form of a shipping margin based upon metric tons loaded. In December 1993, a company called the National Gas Shipping Company (NGSCO) was incorporated and registered in the British Virgin Islands (again with identical ownership to that of ADGAS) to replace the Bermuda-registered LGSC.

In order to ensure the transport of the additional supply produced by the third train expansion project, eight new LNG carriers (each with a capacity of 137,600 cubic meters) were ordered to serve the long-term contracts with Japan. These tankers are still in use today by NGSCO, which also charters LNG, LPG and Sulfur ships to transport ADGAS products to Japan and other parts of the world.

Fiscal Arrangements

ADGAS is subject to taxation in accordance with the fiscal regime governing gas projects. Under this particular fiscal regime, a tax holiday is granted during the first five years from the commencement of commercial production. Thereafter, an income tax of 55 percent is charged. No other taxes are imposed on the company or its shareholders but the agreement does require payment to the government (or its agent, ADNOC) for the gas utilized in the project if the profits exceed a certain defined target operating income (15 percent after tax). No export tax is imposed on products and no customs duties are charged on the goods and equipment imported for the project.

Abu Dhabi Gas Industries Limited (GASCO)

GASCO was established by a joint venture agreement, signed in July 1978, to exploit associated natural gas from onshore fields. After collecting associated gas from the onshore fields of Bu Hasa, Asab, Bab and Sahil, processing is carried out by three processing plants at the fields, where natural gas liquids (NGLs) are extracted and transported by pipeline over a distance of some 220 km to a fractionation plant at Ruwais for the final separation of LPG and Pentane. The fractionation plant, which entered commercial production in February 1982, has the capacity to produce 4.75 million tons per year of finished products, consisting of 1.22 million tons per year of commercial grade Propane; 1.41 million tons per year of Butane; and 2.12 million tons per year of Pentane Plus. The project utilizes 1,030 million cfpd of associated gas as feedstock. From Ruwais, LNG is shipped out to its markets abroad. GASCO is presently planning an expansion of gas processing capacity to handle the additional gas that will be produced once the two onshore gas development projects (AGD-2 and AGD-3) have been completed in 2007–2008.

Management and Administration of GASCO

GASCO is controlled by ADNOC (68 percent holding) with 3 participants—Total, Shell (15 percent each) and Partex (2 percent). The business and affairs of GASCO are managed by a Board of Directors composed of seven Directors, of whom ADNOC appoints four and Total, Shell and Partex each appoint one. The Chairman of the Board is nominated by ADNOC and appointed by the Board from among its members.

Resolutions of the Board are passed with the approval of a Director from ADNOC and a Director appointed by either Total or Shell—except for matters of particular importance, where the approval of all the Directors entitled to vote is required. These matters include, *inter alia*:

- alteration of the articles of association;
- sale, liquidation or renewal of the lifespan of GASCO (30 years);
- alteration of share capital;
- terms and conditions of loans; and
- any expansion of the NGL complex beyond its design capacity, or any change in its scope of operations.

The General Manager is nominated by ADNOC and appointed by the Board according to the terms and conditions that it has approved.

The joint venture agreement is supplemented by a number of additional agreements which include a Gas Supply and Payment Agreement (GSPA) and a Processing and Off-take Agreement.

Under the GSPA, ADNOC agrees to supply to each participant a quantity of associated gas from the oil fields which is equal to each participant's share of the processing capacity of the LNG complex. This is subject to the availability of such quantities of crude oil from the fields and the requirements for use of such quantities determined by the operating company ADCO for the efficient operation of the oil fields.

ADNOC, as owner on behalf of the government and supplier of the gas, is entitled to a gas payment from the participants. However, a participant is not required to make any payment if its actual net operating income in a calendar year is less than 25 percent of its share in the total investment during the five years after commencement of operations, or is less than 15 percent following this period.

The purpose of the Processing and Off-take Agreement is to define arrangements relating to the availability of processing capacity for associated gas, the off-take of the products by the participants and the payment by each participant to GASCO (as an operating company representing the participants) of its processing fee, amounting to the participant's share of GASCO's costs for each calendar year. This agreement confirms GASCO as the processing agent for each participant.

GASCO is not, however, entrusted with the task of marketing the finished products, as this is the responsibility of the joint venture partners, each of which receives an entitlement in proportion to its shareholding. Japan is ADNOC's main market, where it has succeeded in concluding contracts with regular clients for the sale of the bulk of its share of LPG output.

As in the case of ADGAS, a letter from the Department of Petroleum was issued to the shareholders of GASCO (on December 12, 1978) establishing the fiscal arrangements by which the shareholders are bound. Since GASCO is just a processing company for its shareholders and does not independently market the finished products, it does not realize any profits which would be subject to taxation. Unlike ADGAS, which pays income tax on its revenues realized through the sale of its products, GASCO does not pay income tax. Instead, the Abu Dhabi income tax is imposed, in accordance with the Departmental Letter, on each participant of GASCO. If, however, GASCO were to become a profit-making entity, it too would be subject to taxation.

GASCO, with its multinational partners and staff, has been a model of smooth operation and efficient performance, fully repaying all of its ADIA loans by 1992.

Gas Marketing: LPG and LNG Sales Contracts

Gas sales contracts are in many ways unique. They have evolved to reflect the markets in which their commodities are traded and, in certain cases, to shape those markets. During this evolutionary process, gas sales contracts have developed unique characteristics in response to market requirements. Thus, a study of contractual terms can shed light not only on the content of individual contracts, but on the market as a whole. For this reason, the major provisions of both LPG and LNG sales contracts will be reviewed, highlighting those provisions that are truly unique as a result of market demand.

Before embarking on this discussion, it should be noted that the information presented herein will, by necessity, be somewhat general. A specific review of each provision and its origin would require a study beyond the scope of this chapter. In many ways, such an undertaking is not necessary as all contracts are tailored to fit specific market circumstances and the individual needs of a particular buyer and seller. Therefore, the intention is to highlight significant contractual provisions and relate Abu Dhabi's experience in dealing with those provisions.

[98]

Common Features of LPG and LNG Contracts

LPG and LNG contracts share a number of standard terms, many of which appear in virtually all sales contracts. These terms provide the mechanism for the sales relationship and are not product-specific. Their content, however, is usually modified to suit the needs of the individual parties and the gas market.

Far more important in the context of this study are those sections of the sales contracts that rely on the product and its market to shape their content. The most obvious of product-specific terms are, naturally, contained in the section which describes the product itself. Typically, this section will not only set forth the chemical components of the LPG or LNG, but also the acceptable level of impurities and the testing methods used to measure them. Quality specifications are rarely the subject of negotiation, however, as a given gas reserve and the related processing cannot be tailored to individual client needs. Generally, the only differences in these terms in an LPG or LNG contract are those that recognize the chemical differences between the products and the testing methods used.

Although quality specifications may not be subject to negotiation, related warranties occasionally are. LPG and LNG contracts oblige the seller to provide LPG or LNG that conforms to the quality specifications contained in the contract. Typically, it is the purchaser that must decide if the specified quality is suitable for the intended purpose, as only the purchaser is familiar with its production facilities and related fuel needs. For these reasons, the seller may require that the contract contain a provision that specifically disclaims any warranty related to the product. Such a disclaimer of warranty is standard in LPG contracts and a prominent feature of ADNOC's LPG contract.

LNG purchasers have, in certain cases, looked to the seller to provide assurances related to product fitness and a corresponding warranty. From the seller's perspective, however, the reasons for resisting such provisions are the same as for not including them in LPG contracts; the purchaser is in the best position to decide if the quality is suitable for the intended purpose. Nevertheless, in the LNG market, the seller may sometimes agree to a limited warranty of fitness. The issue of warranties is one of many where the product market and the particular relationships in the market specifically impact the contractual terms.

One of the most fundamental aspects of a sales contract is the quantity provision. Unfortunately, in gas sales contracts it can often be difficult to state with precision how much of the product is to be purchased and, while LPG and LNG contracts each have quantity provisions, they are handled in slightly different ways:

LPG Quantity Provisions

An examination of LPG quantity provisions reveals that many are based on two general models. In the first, the contract will specify a given quantity of LPG, either as a total or as Propane and Butane (the primary constituents of LPG), and will allow a fluctuation of plus or minus 10 percent of the specified quantity. Certain limited instances – primarily when the seller is not involved in the transportation of the LPG – allow the buyer to control the fluctuation. It is more common, however, for the seller to act as the final arbiter of the quantity determination. Alternatively, the seller may determine the quantity to be purchased, provided such quantity is within the specified minimum and maximum quantities.

The standard ADNOC LPG Free on Board (FOB)[8] sales contract stipulates individual quantities for Propane and Butane, each of which may be increased or decreased (by ADNOC) by 10 percent. Quantity provisions that provide a seller with significant levels of flexibility recognize that the production of LPG cannot be subject to precise regulation. Often, the source of feedstock for LPG production is crude oil production. These quantity determinations recognize these production realities. Quantity determinations are also indirectly related to shipping terms. For example; ADNOC typically sells LPG on an FOB basis at the plant, meaning that quantity is determined at the time of loading.

LNG Quantity Provisions

Similarly, the quantity provisions of LNG contracts recognize the realities of the LNG marketplace. The need for LNG quantity flexibility is determined by production and demand. LNG production levels during the early years of a contract may be significantly less than those during the mid-to-late years, as the facilities mature and are capable of more efficient operation. Accordingly, contract quantities vary in relation to expected production levels. Typically, this means that the quantity in the first five years of the contract (often referred to as the "build-up period") will gradually increase to a stated level which will remain fixed thereafter. This type of approach has been adopted by ADGAS to accommodate its expansion.

A single contract level would, however, not account for the unpredictability of demand. Most LNG term contract buyers are large utility companies and use the LNG as fuel for producing electricity. As can be expected, demand for electricity (and thus LNG) will vary greatly over the course of a long-term project. Therefore, the contract must accommodate this variance to the satisfaction of both parties. This is generally achieved by providing a base quantity level from which the buyer is afforded upward and downward flexibility. If the buyer does not accept delivery of the base quantity, it is generally required to accept the difference at a later date (although limited exceptions apply). However, the contract will almost always identify a minimum level that must be taken and paid for to guarantee the economic viability of the project.

Less clear, at least in terms of standard contractual provisions, is what happens in the event that production levels provide quantities in excess of the maximum contract quantities. The seller may have complete discretion with respect to such excess quantities for the duration of the contract or for a specified period of time or, alternatively, the buyer may retain the right of first refusal. Generally, in such cases the parties will meet, discuss the possibilities and agree on an appropriate solution.

ADGAS' relationship with its single buyer, TEPCO, has generally followed the features described above. The original plant start-up in 1977 involved a build-up period to reach the full contractual quantities. The expansion of the ADGAS plant and the corresponding increase in output also involved a tiered approach to contractual quantities. Quantity levels were increased during the early years of the contract and eventually reached a plateau for the remaining duration. The contract provided significant quantity flexibility by allowing upward and downward flexibility from the stated quantity levels, although various levels of commitment (including those described as "best efforts") apply in relation to the exercise of such flexibility.

On the technical side – and regardless of product category – a contract must outline the procedures for determining the actual quantity delivered, regardless of the content of the quantity section in general. As with quality specifications, these procedures are developed with operations personnel.

Flexibility in quantities also depends on availability. Most LNG and LPG contracts will provide the seller with some leeway in terms of performance in the event of a gas feedstock supply interruption. Such an event might be caused either by an interruption or reduction in supply (due, for instance, to technical, operational reasons) or as a result of force majeure. A failure or reduction in supply will normally result in a lowering of contract quantities, but the contract remains otherwise valid. In fact, force majeure – which may apply to both parties depending on the event in question – will result in a cessation of deliveries and potentially a cancellation of the contract. In the case of LPG contracts these terms do not pose a significant problem for buyers – as a spot market exists for LPG – but may be of significant importance to sellers because of their dependence on crude oil production for LPG feedstock. This is not the case, however, for LNG. Although a small spot market has developed recently, generally there is still no widespread spot market which could economically satisfy the large scale energy demands of a utility company, so LNG buyers are very concerned with the source of supply and will request assurances of adequate supply and limitations to any contractual excuses to performance.[9]

When it comes to the duration of term contracts the markets for LPG and LNG vary greatly. LPG term contracts today, like most others covering the sale of liquid hydrocarbons, usually cover a period of about one year. This allows both parties to arrange a relationship without the risks associated with extended duration. However, at the time when the GASCO project came on-stream in 1981 and Abu Dhabi entered the LPG market, there was considerable concern about covering project costs in a market that was much less developed in the Gulf than it is today. As a result, Abu Dhabi's first LPG contracts were for a term of five years. This provided a period within which customer relationships could be established with LPG buyers. Over time, the term period was gradually reduced to one year, in line with the current industry standard.

LNG contracts, on the other hand, usually cover a period of twenty to twenty-five years. To explain this extended duration, an examination of the underlying economics is required. LNG projects require immense amounts of upfront capital. Generally, the capital requirement is so large that it can take seven to ten years to repay.

This requires sellers to lock-in demand (sales) for an extended period in order to assure the economic viability of the project as a whole. Without long-term sales commitments, it is extremely difficult to launch an LNG project. Buyers also benefit from the length of the contract. Utility companies require large amounts of cost-efficient fuel for their operations. This type of commodity is increasingly difficult to find in the energy marketplace. By making a long-term commitment, buyers can insulate themselves from supply fluctuations. The long-term nature of LNG contracts therefore benefits both parties. For ADGAS, the initial term of the contractual agreement with TEPCO was twenty years, and the term for the present sales contract which covers the LNG plant after its expansion is twenty-five years.

Dispute Resolution

The contractual mechanisms for resolving problems involving term contracts are as different as the marketplaces for LPG and LNG, and are a direct result of the different contractual periods. As described above, both LPG and LNG contracts provide for formal dispute resolution. In reality, these proceedings are relatively uncommon. There are two types of remedy available to a party if a breach occurs: "contractual" and "at-law." Remedies at-law vary greatly according to which laws are applicable to the contract and are not usually set forth explicitly in the contract itself. However, certain contractual remedies may be used in addition to the solutions provided by the applicable law.

As LPG contracts generally cover shorter periods, a "remedies" section is often included. These contractual remedies range from the cancellation of the contract to an interruption of supply. ADNOC's LPG contracts contain both of these contractual provisions, allowing for either a termination of the contract or the exemption of the seller from its obligation to sell—without relieving the buyer of any of its obligations.

LNG sales contracts generally call for a different approach to contractual remedies. Given the duration of the contract and the mutual desire of the seller and the buyer to preserve good relations, a strict contractual approach to unexpected difficulties would work against the interests of both parties. What has therefore evolved is a "meet and discuss" approach to problem management that invariably revolves around the concepts of "good faith" and mutual cooperation and understanding. Typically titled "Change in Circumstances," this section of the contract may apply – either expressly or implicitly – to all manner of unexpected difficulties ranging from supply problems, delivery scheduling or pricing formulas to any other issue that may arise during the contract period. While this lack of precision may seem incongruous in a sales contract, the flexibility it offers recognizes the mutual benefit of the relationship to both parties and the impossibility of accurately predicting market and other pressures twenty years or more in advance.

Delivery of Gas

Regarding delivery, gas contracts rely on the definitions of the various delivery methods contained in the ICC's Incoterms. This publication is well respected and sets forth in great detail the respective obligations of the parties pursuant to each type of sale, thereby removing the need for the sales contracts to outline the same—provided the ICC Incoterms definitions are expressly incorporated as part of the contract.[10] If the terms of the contract also cover shipping, it must set forth all of the technical provisions related to delivery and scheduling. Generally, LPG is sold "ex-works" or FOB and, as a result, the seller is not involved in transportation; LNG sales are more likely to require the seller to arrange for the transportation of the goods. Having made these generalizations, however, it should be noted that there are also sales of LPG on a cost-and-freight (CFR) basis and sales of LNG on an FOB basis. There is no single accepted standard in gas contracts, so most decisions in this regard are reached either as a result of market conditions unique to the buyer and seller at the time, a corporate decision to sell a certain product on specified terms, or a combination of both. This further demonstrates the ability of gas sales contracts to respond to the marketplace.

Price

While most term contracts include a fixed price for the goods to be sold, this is not the case for gas contracts. A fixed price would not allow the contracts the flexibility to respond quickly and effectively to constant changes in the market. Gas contracts have therefore evolved to include price formulas that take into account a variety factors. To appreciate these formulas, it is first necessary to review some of the relevant aspects of the related markets. Since the markets for LNG and LPG are so different, the prices relating to each will be discussed separately.

LPG Prices

Certain aspects of the LPG market are of particular significance when it comes to pricing. LPG is normally co-produced with crude oil; as a result, production cannot be easily adjusted to meet LPG demand. Furthermore, LPG must be refrigerated or pressurized, making storage costly and surpluses impractical. While certain users – such as utility companies that supply heat to household customers – may be less sensitive to price in the short term, other users – such as petrochemical feedstock buyers of LPG – are very sensitive to price as LPG must compete with other feedstock alternatives. Thus there is no single price at which all available LPG would be purchased by the market since different types of buyers are driven by different economic incentives. While LPG is produced in conjunction with crude oil, there is clearly a distinct LPG market, as illustrated by the fluctuating demand in the spot market.

The traditional LPG pricing mechanism in use in the Arabian Gulf, the world's primary supplier of LPG, did not factor in this notion of a distinct LPG market. LPG prices were indexed solely to Arab light crude oil and the producing nations were free to adjust the price ratio (cost of LPG expressed as a percent of cost of thermal equivalent of Arab light crude oil) while remaining unrestricted by the pricing mechanism. An important aspect of this scheme was the right of the buyer to "phase-out" of the contract. If the price ratio exceeded specified levels or the buyer and seller had not agreed on the appropriate price, the buyer was entitled to gradually decrease its quantity commitment over a suitable period— usually nine months. However, only one of the two scenarios above would be incorporated into the sales contract.

The LPG pricing scheme was dramatically altered in early 1992 by the Saudi state-owned SAMAREC (the Saudi Arabian Marketing and Refining Company, now dissolved and taken over by Saudi Aramco). SAMAREC, the world's largest marketer of LPG, announced a new pricing mechanism that was designed to recognize the market for LPG and capture some of the price differential in spot LPG sales. The new formula set the base LPG price for a given month at 90 percent of the FOB price for the thermal equivalent of Arab light crude oil. To incorporate the spot market, SAMAREC issued a public tender and completed a sale, thereby establishing a spot price. If this spot price differed from the previously determined base price by more than US$15 per ton, 50 percent of the differential was reflected in an adjusted contract price. Furthermore, SAMAREC buyers no longer had a phase-out option within the new pricing formula.

While ADNOC has not specifically integrated this pricing formula into its standard contracts, the prices resulting from it do impact the ADNOC price. ADNOC's standard LPG contract for FOB sales includes a mechanism that determines prices by referring to "arm's length"[11] prices in the Arabian Gulf for similar products (in terms of quantity and quality) sold pursuant to similar terms. Thus, assuming otherwise similar terms, the ADNOC formula includes the SAMAREC price as a reference, and as a result recognizes the LPG market. ADNOC's LPG contracts also contain a modified take-or-pay provision dealing with failure to lift in certain circumstances. In essence, the buyer is required to pay when, through no fault of the seller or force majeure, the buyer fails to lift (take delivery of) the contracted quantities of LPG.

LNG Prices

While LNG price formulae have responded to markets, this has largely involved guarantees of demand rather than price modifications. As mentioned earlier, continued, consistent sales are the single most important concern for LNG producers. Thus, the producers cannot be subject to the uncertainties of market demand and require a contractual commitment of a specified minimum volume in order to ensure the required levels of cash flow—which are particularly important for projects that require commercial financing. This type of contractual commitment is referred to as "take-or-pay" (i.e., even if buyers do not take delivery of the minimum quantity, they must pay for it). Beyond this minimum quantity, buyers are generally entitled to a degree of quantity flexibility as discussed above, but the take-or-pay obligation is of paramount importance to producers as it effectively shifts demand risk to the purchaser of LNG. Take-or-pay provisions therefore can influence LNG pricing and lessen the risk to producers posed by fluctuating crude oil prices that are a component of the overall LNG pricing scheme. Alternatively, producers might prefer a fixed LNG price to guarantee a reliable minimum cash flow.

It is equally important that LNG competes in the energy marketplace with other sources of energy. In most of the relevant sectors, gas can either replace, or be replaced by, competing energy sources. This fact means that LNG must be priced competitively, but not independently from other fuels. Numerous contractual mechanisms have been developed to incorporate the concept of competitive inter-fuel pricing into the relationship between buyer and seller. These mechanisms allow the price of LNG to fluctuate in response to the market price of competing fuels and effectively shift the risk associated with changing prices to the seller.

Current LNG pricing provides for a floating price that is tied to some form of indicator designed to fluctuate with changes in the market price of competing fuels. While workable, this practice raises an additional issue; should the indicator relate to the export market of the seller or the import market of the purchaser? No standard practice currently exists, however, and therefore this decision is wholly dependent upon the type of sale and the particular markets involved.

The indicator must rely on reputable publications that accurately report prices, and must consider contingencies in case the primary reference publication is discontinued. Most importantly, the indicator must gauge the right competing product. Today, most LNG prices are linked to crude oil. At some point in the future crude oil may no longer be a functional reference point if the LNG trade develops into a self-referencing market (regard the evolution of LPG pricing, for example) but, for now, this link is acceptable to buyers and sellers and provides a workable reference.

Certain price terms may also contain a market re-negotiation clause. This allows the parties to adjust their agreement to meet evolving market conditions and may contain triggers that allow re-negotiation upon the occurrence of certain events or which come into operation at specified time intervals. These clauses are designed to allow the contracting parties to respond to the unexpected (this goal may also be met via the "change in circumstances" provision of the contract). In fact, even in the absence of a market re-negotiation mechanism, the mutual benefit of the economic success of both buyer and seller is likely to drive the desire for re-negotiation in the presence of truly unexpected market forces. Following this model of flexibility, numerous large LNG contracts have been re-negotiated to secure both parties a better deal.

Government regulation can also affect the price of LNG through molding policies towards the fulfillment of national interests and priorities. Government regulation in Abu Dhabi, however, is not a significant factor in formulating an LNG price framework.

In Abu Dhabi, since ADGAS commenced operations in 1977, LNG (and LPG) has been delivered to TEPCO. The original 1972 agreement with TEPCO set the delivered price for the LNG in Japan at slightly less than US$1 per million British thermal units (Btu). After negotiations, a revised sales agreement was concluded between TEPCO and ADGAS in 1976. The new agreement provided for an increase in the initial delivered cost, insurance and freight (CIF) price for the LNG to $2 per million Btu. Through subsequent negotiations Abu Dhabi linked its gas prices to those of oil. From the start of 1980 it was agreed to index the LNG price against Abu Dhabi's Murban crude. Thus in 1980, the price of the equivalent of 1 million Btu rose from $5.04 to $5.75. However, it is worth mentioning that on a heating value basis, despite this sharp rise, LNG was still cheaper than competitive crude.

In 1988 the method used to fix the price of ADGAS LNG was revised once again. A formula was adopted which was similar to that being used by other projects selling LNG to Japan. One basic element of the formula linked the price of LNG to a basket of crude imported into Japan, commonly known as the "Japanese Crude Cocktail." This element of the formula was based on a three-month average CIF price for the Japanese Crude Cocktail. Additional adjustments where then made, taking into account certain agreed factors. Because a portion of the adjustment is periodically reviewed within certain parameters, the net effect of the pricing formula is a workable price for both parties that reflects ongoing market conditions.

On the whole, gas contracts have responded remarkably well to market conditions. By adapting to the market, gas contracts have provided a product conduit to the marketplace. It is by facilitating, rather than hindering (as contracts are often accused of) this profitable trade that gas contracts have proved their usefulness.

5

The Tax System Applicable
to Petroleum Operations in Abu Dhabi

There is no special tax legislation applicable to the oil industry in Abu Dhabi. Income tax is imposed by the Abu Dhabi Income Tax Decree of 1965. This decree was not promulgated specifically as a piece of petroleum tax legislation but as a corporate tax law of general application, although the Decree contains certain provisions related to oil operations (this is to be expected, as the oil industry provides the country's most important source of income). In practice, however, these provisions are only applicable to companies "dealing in petroleum" (i.e., dealing with the production and export of petroleum) and to petrochemical companies and branches of foreign banks. The tax rate defined by the Decree varies according to the level of taxable income. The rate applicable to income derived from oil activities was initially fixed at 50 percent, but was raised in 1971 to 55 percent, which was thereafter considered the minimum income tax rate for oil operations.

Amendments to the Tax Decree

The first amendment to the tax Decree was introduced in 1966 (Abu Dhabi Income Tax [Amendment] Decree 1966) and came into force on January 1, 1966. The purpose of the amendment was to provide for the "expensing of royalty." OPEC, using its collective bargaining power, secured the approval of the oil companies in the Middle East in 1964–1965 to apply this concept in the producing countries of the region—Abu Dhabi's 1966 amendment was issued for this purpose.

In 1970 two partial amendments were introduced to the income tax decree. The first amendment dealt with "expenses deemed to be capital expenses by an agreement between the Ruler and the chargeable person."[1] The second amendment aimed to confirm that the royalty to be expensed was not just the royalty as it stood when this concept was introduced in 1966 (equal to 12.5 percent of the value of the crude petroleum) but also any "royalty of greater amount as may from time to time be agreed between the Ruler and such producing company."[2]

In 1971, a fourth amendment was adopted (Abu Dhabi Income Tax [Amendment] Decree, issued on February 5, 1971) which raised the rate of income tax from 50 percent to 55 percent. This was the result of a collective decision made by the OPEC member countries:

> In early 1971, negotiations between OPEC and the oil companies began in Tehran and Tripoli with the aim of establishing a five-year price pact for the period 1971 to 1976. Threatening to embargo any company not acceding to its demands, OPEC forced through an initial increase in the tax reference price from US$ 1.80 to US$ 2.18, coupled with a tax rate increase from 50 to 55 per cent.[3]

In 1974, OPEC members decided to increase the rate of income tax applicable to the "major" oil concessions to 85 percent (and to increase the royalty to 20 percent), which became known as the "OPEC Formula."[4] In implementing this decision, the Chairman of the Abu Dhabi Petroleum Department addressed a letter (No. AD-1/18/1507) on November 14, 1974 to ADPC and ADMA stating: "it is decided to increase the rate of income tax on the oil companies' profits to 85 percent with effect from 1st November 1974."[5] (The rate of royalty was increased to 20 percent also with effect from November 1, 1974.)

This increase in the Abu Dhabi income tax rate – unlike the previous amendments to the income tax decree in 1966, 1970 and 1971 and the increase of the income tax rate to 55 percent in 1971, all of which were effected by a decree from the Ruler – took the form of a letter from the Chairman of the Abu Dhabi Petroleum Department addressed to the concerned oil companies. Some have therefore questioned the legal validity of the increase in the income tax rate (although the two oil companies concerned – ADPC and ADMA – never objected formally to its implementation and never questioned its legal validity. On the contrary, it was followed by them when preparing their annual income tax declarations).

There are, however, no grounds to question the validity of the increase as the method of implementation was merely a result of a change that occurred in 1974 concerning the re-organization of government machinery in the emirate of Abu Dhabi.

As mentioned earlier, the Abu Dhabi Petroleum Department was created and was entrusted with all matters concerning the petroleum industry in Abu Dhabi. In light of the powers granted to the Petroleum Department, it is not unreasonable that a decision to increase the income tax rate for oil companies (in implementing the decisions of OPEC and the oil ministers of the region) took the form of a letter from the Chairman of this department (on behalf of the government). Indeed, the oil concession agreements which were concluded between Abu Dhabi and the oil companies in the period 1980–1981 were not signed by the Ruler but by a representative of the government who was, in most cases, the Chairman of the Petroleum Department. Furthermore, the fiscal regimes applicable to the two gas companies in Abu Dhabi – ADGAS and GASCO – were established (in 1977 and 1978 respectively) by a letter from the Petroleum Department, and the fixed margin of profit for the oil companies (starting at $0.22 per barrel in 1979 and later increasing to $1.00 per barrel) was initially approved and later changed by a decision of the Petroleum Department.[6]

For the smaller concessions the rate of income tax (and royalty) varies from one to another. The Abu Dhabi authorities have, in effect, accepted the idea that the smaller, high-cost oil fields – particularly those offshore – require some relief from the standard OPEC rate, which was designed for large-scale ventures. When reviewing the small concessions granted in the period 1967–1971 one will notice that, for instance, the Abu Dhabi Oil Company (Japan) Ltd. pays 55 percent tax and a 12.5 percent royalty; Total Abu Al Bukoosh pays 75 percent tax and a 20 percent royalty; Al-Bunduq Company also pays 75 percent tax and a 20 percent royalty; and Amerada Hess, before relinquishing its concession to the Abu Dhabi government in the late 1990s, paid a tax of 55 percent and a royalty on a sliding scale from 12.5 percent to 16 percent according to its production level. ADNOC is also subject to the income tax decree. According to Article 9 of the law establishing ADNOC (Law No. 7 of 1971, dated November 27, 1971), the company must pay the government 55 percent of its annual net profits (which was the rate applicable to oil companies in 1971).[7]

The new model of concession agreement, concluded in 1980–1981 (as represented by the Deminex concession agreement of 1981) has generally adopted an income tax rate increasing progressively or on a sliding scale basis from 55 percent to 85 percent as the volume of production rises—a sliding scale royalty is also generally applicable, ranging from 12.5 percent to 20 percent, as the level of production increases (see Articles 17 and 18 of the Deminex Agreement – Appendix IV – dealing with taxation).

For industrial projects based on gas (ADGAS, GASCO and the Ruwais Fertilizer Project) a special fiscal regime has been conceived which is much more favorable to them than the general system applicable to the oil companies (in order to encourage the exploitation of natural gas resources and attract the heavy investments required).

As mentioned earlier, this particular regime stipulates that the gas company is subject to the Abu Dhabi Income Tax Decree of 1965 (as amended) but enjoys a tax holiday during the first five years from the commencement of commercial production. Thereafter, "the Company shall be liable for Abu Dhabi income tax at a rate of 55 percent of profits" (with the possibility of carrying forward any loss incurred for not more than five consecutive years from the end of the income tax year in which such loss is incurred).

Other than income tax no other taxes are imposed on the company or its shareholders but payments must be made to the government on the gas utilized in the project if the profits exceed a certain defined target operating income (i.e., 15 percent after tax).

This special fiscal regime applicable to gas companies is usually presented in a letter issued by the SPC (formerly the Abu Dhabi Petroleum Department) to the shareholders of the proposed gas project. This letter is therefore referred to in the petroleum industry of Abu Dhabi as the "Departmental Letter."

In 1979, the concept of a fixed margin of profits for ADPC and ADMA (which were subject to income tax at a rate of 85 percent and a royalty of 20 percent) was introduced in Abu Dhabi to ensure the profitability of their operations and to assure the shareholders of both companies of the competitiveness of dealing in Abu Dhabi oil compared to other sources. A letter (No. M-1-3-533, dated February 19, 1979) from the Chairman of the Petroleum Department to ADMA Ltd., reads:

> We refer to your letter dated January 31st, 1979 in respect of the financial position of your Company and we wish to inform you that the Government approves the principle of a fixed profit for your company of 22 American cents per barrel after payment of tax for petroleum produced.[8]

It is clear from the wording of this letter that this "fixed margin" is a post-tax relief to the shareholders of ADMA to ensure the competitiveness of their oil operations in Abu Dhabi. It is quite independent of the calculation of Abu Dhabi tax and should not, therefore, affect the basis of taxation. This special treatment was later extended to ADPC and the "fixed margin" gradually increased until it reached its present amount of $1.00 per barrel.

Fixing the Price of Oil for Tax or Other Purposes[9]

The old-style concession agreements stipulated a payment of royalty charges on each ton of oil produced, regardless of its sale price or the profit realized from it, indicating that governments were not really interested in the price at which the oil was sold.

Then, in 1950–1951, certain oil producing countries in the Middle East (Saudi Arabia, Iraq and Kuwait) adopted the profit-sharing principle (Abu Dhabi adopted the same principle in 1966). According to this principle, the host government's share moved from a fixed royalty per unit of production or export to 50 percent of the net company profit based on posted prices. When the new financial arrangement was adopted, the host countries became directly affected by the posted price (which was a tax reference price used for the calculation of the companies' profits and did not always reflect market realities). In that period, and until the early 1970s, the posted prices of crude oil were determined by the oil companies alone without any consultation with the host countries.

In February 1959, the oil companies decided, without prior consultation with the governments concerned, to cut the price of Middle Eastern Oil by about 18 cents per barrel. In spite of the uproar that the companies' action provoked, they went on to cut prices again in August 1960 by an average of about 9 cents per barrel. It is generally recognized that the successive unilateral cuts in oil prices by the major oil companies in 1959 and 1960 were the catalysts for the creation of OPEC in September 1960.

One of the original principal aims of OPEC was to stabilize oil prices. Article 2 (B) of OPEC's statute states: "The Organization shall devise ways and means of ensuring the stabilization of prices in international markets with a view to eliminating harmful and unnecessary fluctuations." The first success achieved by OPEC in this regard was the freezing of oil prices at the post-August 1960 level. In a further attempt to strengthen prices and discourage the granting of large discounts by oil companies, the OPEC Conference recommended in April 1966 that the governments of member countries should apply posted prices or reference prices for the purpose of determining the tax liabilities of the oil companies operating in their territories.

In terms of royalties paid by the oil companies, in 1962 OPEC recommended that the member countries increase the royalty rate and adopt the principle of royalty expensing. According to the 50–50 profit-sharing formula introduced in 1950–1951, royalties, which usually amounted to 12.5 percent of the posted price multiplied by the number of barrels produced, were considered a credit towards the 50 percent income tax liability of the companies instead of being treated as an expense. Although OPEC failed in its attempts to achieve an increase in the royalty rate of 12.5 percent it succeeded in having royalties expensed in 1964.

After the outbreak of the October 1973 Arab–Israeli War, the Arabian Gulf oil ministers met in Kuwait on 16 October and decided to fix oil prices themselves, unilaterally. Essentially they decided to substitute legislation for negotiation. They seized the initiative to formulate their own oil policy in pricing and settling production levels. This established a new principle in the oil industry: oil pricing was to be decided upon by the host countries and not by the oil companies operating therein. At that meeting the posted price of the Saudi 34° marker oil, FOB Ras Tanura, was raised from \$3.001 to \$5.119 per barrel. The price of Abu Dhabi Murban 39° thus moved up from \$3.144 to \$ 6.045.

On December 22–23 the Gulf members of OPEC met in Tehran and decided to raise posted prices to a much higher level—in view of later developments in the oil market. They set the new posting for the Saudi marker crude at \$11.65, effective from January 1, 1974. Since that time it has been the policy and practice of the OPEC member counties to fix the price of their oil themselves, for tax purposes or otherwise, but not in an arbitrary manner. Oil prices are determined by market forces through supply and demand. The price of Abu Dhabi Murban 39° therefore moved up to \$12.636 (on January 1, 1974). It is interesting to note that the price of this crude by January 2007 stood at \$54.85.

One of the main aims of OPEC's pricing strategy is to ensure the stability of the oil market. OPEC's Economic Commission Board used to meet on a quarterly basis to determine and recommend to the member countries posted prices for each quarter, taking into account all relevant factors. However, in the mid-1980s those quarterly meetings stopped, and each member country began to determine the posted prices of its oil in light of market conditions.

6

The Settlement of Disputes under Petroleum Agreements

As a general rule, oil concessions in the Middle East dictate that disputes between the concessionaire and the producing country which cannot be settled by negotiation or mutual agreement should be resolved by arbitration. This provision appeared in the text of the first oil concession granted in the Middle East in 1901 to the D'Arcy Exploration Company by the Persian government and has appeared in most concession agreements concluded since.

Arbitration is more attractive to its proponents in the business community – including in domestic disputes – than other methods of dispute resolution (e.g., judicial litigation) as it can be quicker, cheaper, less formal and offer more privacy than litigation. It also allows the parties to control the course of the proceedings and to choose the law which is to be applied, based on the particular characteristics of the dispute. In cases of disputes that include an international element, there is yet another advantage—arbitration secures a neutral venue for the settlement of disputes and a neutrally appointed tribunal, independent from the national court of either party.

As a result of this requirement of neutrality of venue and tribunal, arbitration assumes even greater significance when a company has entered into a relationship with a foreign government—as in an oil concession. A party which lodges a claim against a state in that state's own courts may fear that the ruling will not be impartial. Likewise, states are generally reluctant to agree to adjudication in the courts of countries other than their own (e.g., the courts of the concessionaire's country).

Fuad Rouhani, the first Secretary-General of OPEC, explains the reasons behind the adoption of the arbitral concept in oil concessions:

> [I]n general, there is considerable international support for the opinion that for the settlement of trade disputes arbitration is preferable to judicial procedure even where domestic differences are concerned, for reasons which seem to be universally recognized; arbitration is less rigid, less costly, and less dilatory than the normal judicial procedure. Furthermore, persons who invest capital on a large scale in a foreign country feel more secure having an assurance that, if a dispute arose between them and the host country, they would not be subject to the strict legal system of the country, of which they are often ignorant, and which they may fear may be applied with less than complete impartiality in cases involving foreigners.[1]

It is well known that petroleum investments require large amounts of capital and advanced technology and that the element of risk, which is usually borne by the foreign oil company, is very high. On the other hand, petroleum resources and their development are of vital importance to the economic growth of the producing country, often representing the cornerstone of the country's economic development. Furthermore, petroleum is strategically important for both consuming and producing countries, which explains why oil agreements have often been politically charged in the past. Collectively, these considerations indicate that international arbitration is the most appropriate method for the settlement of disputes which arise between the government of a producing country (or its national oil company) and a foreign oil concessionaire.

The cumulative effect of these advantages can be seen in the determined efforts of those negotiating oil concessions in the Middle East to adopt international arbitration as the preferred method for settling disputes that may arise between parties bound by petroleum agreements. There are, however, a few exceptions where petroleum agreements have provided for recourse to local courts for the settlement of disputes. Indeed, OPEC supports national courts as a forum for the settlement of oil disputes as opposed to international arbitration.

The late Dr. Ibrahim Shihata, former Senior Vice-President and General Counsel of the World Bank, provides an interesting explanation for certain countries' recourse to local courts rather than international arbitration. He writes:

> The reticence of a number of oil-producing countries with respect to international arbitration is explained in part by previous experiences. [On] various occasions, for example, despite contractual clauses providing for the contrary, international arbitral tribunals have discarded the application of municipal law in favor of international law, sometimes using clearly offensive arguments. In one case involving Abu Dhabi, for example, Lord Asquith argued that: "If a national law must be applied, it is that of Abu Dhabi. But no such law can reasonably be said to exist. The Sheikh administers a purely discretionary justice with the assistance of the Koran; and it would be fanciful to suggest that in this very primitive region, there is any set or body of legal principles applicable to the construction of modern commercial instruments."[2]

Similarly, regarding disputes in Qatar, Sir Alfred Bucknill found that there was "no settled body of legal principles in Qatar applicable to the construction of modern commercial instruments."[3]

Recourse to international arbitration certainly remains the preferred method of dispute resolution in petroleum agreements, while those which advocate local courts are becoming rare. A review undertaken by the Secretariat of the International Center for the Settlement of Investment Disputes (ICSID) of 102 oil agreements concluded by 92 different countries indicated that 93 percent of the contracts provided for arbitration (institutional or ad hoc) and only 7 percent provided for recourse to local courts.[4]

Development of Arbitration Clauses

When studying the arbitration clauses in petroleum agreements one cannot fail to notice a clear development, over time, in their drafting and contents. The early oil concessions embodied a simple, though obviously deficient arbitration clause. The D'Arcy concession of 1901, for example, stated in Article 17 that in the event of a dispute or difference arising regarding the interpretation of the concession or the rights or responsibilities of either party, such dispute or difference would be submitted to two arbitrators in Tehran – one named by each of the parties – and to an umpire, who was to be appointed by the arbitrators. Furthermore, the decision of the arbitrators – or in the event of their disagreement, that of the umpire – was to be considered final.[5]

However, this type of clause had several weaknesses which made the arbitration process susceptible to frustration by either of the parties. For instance, it contained no time limits, no indication of what was to be done in the event of refusal by any party to appoint its arbitrator, no provision covering disagreements regarding the appointment of an umpire and no mention of the procedure to be followed or of the law to be applied by the arbitration tribunal. It could almost be said that the provision simply embodied an expression of intent – rather than a formal agreement – to arbitrate.

The Turkish Petroleum Company (later IPC) concession with Iraq in 1925 represented a slight improvement on the D'Arcy concession. Article 40 of the agreement stipulated that if the arbitrators failed to agree upon a referee they were to request that the President of the Permanent Court of International Justice (PCIJ) make the appointment.[6] Again, no provision was made for cases where one of the two parties failed to appoint an arbitrator or where the parties failed to deliver a unified request to the President of the PCIJ to appoint the referee.

The concession granted to AIOC in 1933 included a partial remedy for the deficiencies in the arbitration clauses in use in the oil agreements of the time. In Article 22 it envisaged the case where one of the parties did not appoint its arbitrator, or where the two arbitrators could not agree on the appointment of an umpire, and stipulated that in such cases the appointment would be made by the President of the PCIJ.[7] The same article also indicated the procedure to be followed and the law to be applied by the arbitration tribunal. However, subsequent concessions did not all follow the improved clause embodied in the AIOC agreement, opting instead to use the older, less advanced type of arbitration clause. Such was the case, for example, in the concession granted to Petroleum Development (Trucial Coast) Ltd. (later known as Abu Dhabi Petroleum Company Ltd.—ADPC) in Abu Dhabi in 1939. Article 15 of this agreement, dealing with the settlement of disputes, reads as follows:

> (a) If at any time during the currency of this Agreement there should be any difference or dispute between the two parties as to the interpretation or execution of any provision thereof, or anything herein contained or in connection herewith, such dispute shall be referred to two arbitrators, one selected by each of the two parties, and a referee to be chosen by the arbitrators before proceeding to arbitration.

> (b) Each party shall nominate its arbitrator within sixty days after the delivery of a request so to do by the other party, failing which its arbitrator may, at the request of the other party, be designated by the British Political Resident in the Persian Gulf. In the event of the arbitrators failing to agree upon the referee within sixty days of being chosen or designated, the British Political Resident in the Persian Gulf may appoint a referee at the request of the arbitrators or of either of them.

(c) The decision of the arbitrators, or in case of a difference of opinion between them the decision of the referee, shall be final and binding on both parties.

(d) In giving a decision the arbitrators or the referee shall specify an adequate period of delay during which the party against whom the decision is given shall conform thereto, and that party shall be in default only if he has failed to conform to the decision prior to the expiry of that period, and not otherwise.

(e) The place of arbitration shall be such as may be agreed by the parties, and in default of agreement shall be London or Baghdad.[8]

It is noteworthy that, among other things, this clause does not indicate the procedure to be followed or the law to be applied by the arbitration tribunal. Later in this chapter this clause will be compared to the arbitration clause adopted in the oil concession agreement concluded by Abu Dhabi in the early 1980s.

By far the most elaborate arbitration article in this area of the world appeared in the Iranian consortium agreement concluded in 1954 after the failed attempt to nationalize Iranian oil. This agreement introduced for the first time a comprehensive and carefully worded arbitration clause obviously designed to be less liable to frustration by either party. Article 44 of the agreement stated that arbitration would be the sole method of determining any dispute between the parties and laid down detailed rules governing the arbitration of disputes. The arbitration clause developed in the consortium's agreement was widely adopted in subsequent oil agreements made by Iran.

In 1971 the agreement between NIOC and Amerada Hess expressly provided for the laws of Iran to apply (Article 38). Likewise, the consortium agreement of 1973 also referred to the laws of Iran.

The concessions granted in Libya were all subject to the arbitration provisions laid down in the Libyan Petroleum Law of

1955. From the review of the arbitration clauses in the petroleum agreements referred to above – particularly the old-style concession agreements – one sees that those clauses were generally ad hoc arbitration clauses (as opposed to institutional arbitration). However there is a trend now in modern petroleum agreements towards the adoption of institutional arbitration. In the words of one author:

> With the growth and refinement of arbitration systems ... drafters now have available various comprehensive sets of international arbitration rules and arbitral institutions that have stood the test of time. These can be incorporated by reference into agreements by means of submission clauses that are relatively simple and yet generally superior, in a technical sense, because of the quality of the rules they incorporate. Such institutions include the ICSID and the ICC International Court of Arbitration.[9]

In the review conducted by the ICSID referred to above, it was found that 48 percent of the contracts reviewed provided for institutional arbitration, compared to 45 percent which referred to ad hoc mechanisms (47 percent of the agreements which provided for institutional arbitration specified the ICC as the arbitral forum, 41 percent specified the ICSID and 12 percent specified other types of institutional arbitration). About half of the agreements that provided for ad hoc international arbitration selected the arbitration rules of the UN Commission on International Trade Law (UNCITRAL) as the rules applicable to the procedure.

The general practice followed in the Middle East of envisaging arbitration for the settlement of all disputes between the parties under oil concessions has not been followed in concessions concluded since the 1960s in Egypt and Saudi Arabia. Generally, in the past, Egyptian oil concessions embodied an arbitration clause covering all kinds of disputes. However, the agreements made between Egypt and Pan American in 1963 and 1964 followed a different course. They made a distinction between the concessionaire's disputes with the government and the concessionaire's disputes with the Egyptian Petroleum Corporation (EGPC). The agreements provided that any dispute arising between the government and the parties with respect to the interpretation, application or execution of the agreement should be referred to the appropriate Egyptian courts with competent jurisdiction, but that any disputes arising between Pan American and EGPC should be referred to arbitration. In the event that any party failed to appoint an arbitrator, or if the two arbitrators failed to select a third arbitrator, an application would then be made to the International Chamber of Commerce (ICC) International Court of Arbitration to make such an appointment, with the arbitration being held in Stockholm, Sweden (Article 42).

Saudi Arabia has also shown since the 1960s a disinclination to include an arbitral provision in its contracts. On June 25, 1963, the Council of Ministers issued a decision which limited the government's power to insert an arbitration clause in its contracts to exceptional cases. This attitude was reflected in the oil concession granted by Saudi Arabia to Auxirap on April 4, 1965. In this agreement, Saudi Arabia followed the precedent set in Egypt by making a distinction between the concessionaire's disputes with the government and the concessionaire's dispute with the national oil corporation with which it had entered into a joint venture agreement. Only disputes occurring between Auxirap and PETROMIN (the Saudi national oil corporation) qualified for arbitration in accordance with Article 13 of the agreement.[10]

Cases Successfully Referred to Arbitration

Despite the frequent use of arbitration clauses in oil concessions in the Middle East, in practice only a very small number of disputes have been settled by arbitration. Differences arising between host countries and concessionaires have usually been settled through negotiations. In fact, until the late 1970s, arbitration provisions in oil concessions in the Arab producing countries of the area had been utilized effectively in only four cases, between: the Ruler of Qatar and Petroleum Development (Qatar), Ltd. in 1950; the Sheikh of Abu Dhabi and Petroleum Development (Trucial Coast), Ltd. in 1951; the Ruler of Qatar and the International Marine Oil Company Ltd. in 1953; and the Government of Saudi Arabia and the Arabian American Oil Company (Aramco) in 1958. In the early 1980s there was also an arbitration case involving the government of Kuwait and the American Independent Oil Company (AMINOIL) (1982).

For a complete picture of oil arbitration in the Arab world, one must include the arbitration cases which were filed against the Libyan government by the oil companies that were nationalized by Libya in the 1970s. The arbitrator in the case brought by the Libyan American Oil Company (LIAMCO) against the Government of the Libyan Arab Republic (1977) was Dr. Sobhi Mohmassani, an eminent Lebanese jurist and Professor of Law.

The following is a summary of the arbitration cases referred to above.[11]

Petroleum Development (Qatar) Ltd. vs. Ruler of Qatar (1950)

On May 17, 1935, the Ruler of Qatar entered into a written agreement whereby he granted exclusive mineral rights to APOC. In 1946, APOC assigned its rights and obligations to Petroleum Development Ltd. In June 1949, a dispute occurred regarding the extent of the area that was subject to the rights granted by the 1935 agreement.

Object of the Claim: To determine the extent of the area that was subject to the rights granted by the concession agreement.

Relevant Legal Issues: The award, as reported, was limited to the decision without any indication of the reasoning on which it was based.

Decision: The tribunal held that the concession included islands, over which the Sheikh ruled on the date of the concession; the bed and subsoil of all the inland or national waters of the islands and of the mainland of the State of Qatar and the seabed and subsoil beneath the territorial waters of the island and the main land of the State of Qatar. The tribunal, however, determined that the concession did not include the seabed or subsoil beneath the high seas of the Arabian Gulf contiguous to the territorial waters. [12]

Petroleum Development Ltd. vs. Sheikh of Abu Dhabi, 1951

On January 11, 1939, Sheikh Shakhbut of Abu Dhabi entered into a written contract with Petroleum Development Ltd. whereby the Sheikh granted the company the exclusive right to drill for, discover and produce mineral oil within a certain area in Abu Dhabi. In 1949, the Sheikh purported to transfer mineral rights, acquired as a result of a 1949 proclamation, concerning the continental shelf areas, to a US company. Petroleum Development claimed that the Sheikh could not do so because these rights were granted to them under the terms of the 1939 agreement.

Object of the Claim: The arbitration was to determine the rights of the company with respect to all underwater areas over which the Ruler had or may have had sovereignty (continental shelf and seabed).

Relevant Legal Issues: On the question of the "proper law" that was applicable in construing the contract; the arbitrator held that this was a contract "made in Abu Dhabi and wholly to be performed in that country."[13] Therefore, "if any municipal system of law were applicable, it would prima facie be that of Abu Dhabi." However, the tribunal found that no such a law could "reasonably be said to exist" because the Sheikh administered "a purely discretionary justice with the assistance of the Koran, and it would be fanciful to suggest that in this very primitive region there is any settled body of legal principles applicable to the construction of modern commercial instruments." According to the arbitrator the agreement called "for the application of principles rooted in the good sense and common practice of the generality of civilized nations—a sort of *modern law of nature*." In the view of Lord Asquith, although English municipal law was inapplicable as such, some of its rules were "so firmly grounded in reason as to form part of this broad part of jurisprudence – this modern law of nature …"[14]

Decision: The arbitrator found that the contract included the subsoil of the territorial waters of Abu Dhabi, but not the subsoil of the continental shelf. [15]

Ruler of Qatar vs. International Marine Oil Company Ltd., 1953

A concession agreement was signed on August 5, 1949 between the Ruler of Qatar – the father of the claimant – and agents of the respondent. Under the terms of the agreement, the company was to pay annually an agreed amount of money.

Object of the Claim: The crucial question in this arbitration was whether the proper law to be applied in the construction of the principal agreement was Islamic law or the principles of natural justice and equity. The tribunal observed that there was nothing in the principal or supplemental agreements which shed "clear light upon the intention of the parties on this point." In the view of the referee, all considerations pointed to the application of Islamic law (that being the law administered in Qatar). However, the referee concluded, based on the Abu Dhabi award, that there was "no settled body of legal principles in Qatar applicable to the construction of modem commercial instruments." The arbitrator observed that if Islamic law was applicable, certain parts of the contract would then be "open to the criticism of being invalid." In this respect, the referee added: "I cannot think that the ruler intended Islamic law to apply to a contract upon which he was to receive considerable sums of money, although Islamic law would declare that the transaction was wholly or partially void." It was held that neither party "intended Islamic law to apply," and therefore the agreement was to be governed by the "principles of justice, equity and good conscience."[16]

Decision: On the question of whether the fixed annual payments were payable in arrears or in advance, Sir Alfred Bucknill held that "they were payable in arrear and subject to the right of the Company to terminate its liability in respect thereof after three months' notice."[17]

Saudi Arabia vs. Arabian American Oil Company (Aramco), 1958[18]

On May 29, 1933, a concession agreement was signed between the Government of the Kingdom of Saudi Arabia and Standard Oil Company of California (SOCAL, later Aramco). On January 20, 1954, a different agreement was signed between the Government of the Kingdom of Saudi Arabia and Mr. A.S. Onassis, whereby the Saudi Arabian Maritime Tankers Company Ltd. was to have a right of priority for the transport of oil. Shortly after, Aramco was advised that the Saudi tankers would have priority over its tankers for loading Saudi petroleum. Aramco claimed that the agreement with Mr. Onassis violated the 1933 concession.

Object of the Claim: The arbitration was to determine whether the 1933 concession agreement entitled the company to deny preference or priority to national tankers; and whether the agreement between the Government of the Kingdom of Saudi Arabia and Onassis was in conflict with the Aramco concession agreement. No damages were claimed.

Relevant Legal Issues: The tribunal observed that Saudi Arabian law was chosen by the parties as the applicable law "in so far as matters within the jurisdiction of Saudi Arabia." As to matters beyond the jurisdiction of Saudi Arabia, the parties envisaged the application of a law to be determined by the tribunal.[19]

- Applicable Law: *Lex Arbitri*: Based on the fact that "the Parties ... intended from the very beginning to withdraw their disputes from the jurisdiction of local tribunals," the tribunal held that the law to be applied was "not the law of Saudi Arabia." The arbitrators observed that arbitral proceedings to which a state is a party could not be subject to the law of another state. It was held that the "arbitration, as such," was to be governed by "the Law of Nations."[20]

- Characterization: It was determined by the arbitrators that the oil concession was to be characterized in accordance with Muslim law. The Hanbali School of Muslim law was to determine the legal nature of the concession.

- Proper Law: The tribunal held that: "Matters pertaining to private law are, in principle, governed by the law of Saudi Arabia but with one important reservation. The law must, in case of need, be interpreted or supplemented by the general principles of law, by the custom and practice in the oil business and by notions of pure jurisprudence."[21]

"Contractual Concessions" and "Public Service Concessions": The tribunal held that a concession that is contractual in character gives rights and obligations to the concessionary company that cannot be modified without the company's consent.

Decision: The tribunal found that the Aramco concession was contractual in character, and that its transport provisions were to prevail over those of the Onassis agreement. The tribunal held that Aramco had the exclusive right to transport the oil in question.[22]

Government of Kuwait vs. American Independent Oil Company (AMINOIL), 1982[23]

In 1948 the Government of Kuwait granted to the American Independent Oil Company (AMINOIL) an oil concession in the Kuwait–Saudi Arabia neutral zone. After several modifications of the agreement in the following years, the Gulf states adopted the "Abu Dhabi" formula in 1974, providing for further increases in tax and royalty rates. The parties were unable to agree upon a new scheme of payment. On September 19, 1977, the Government of Kuwait promulgated Decree Law No. 124, which terminated the AMINOIL concession and nationalized all AMINOIL assets in Kuwait. This law provided for the assessment of compensation due to the company by a committee appointed by the government.

Object of the Claim: The Government of Kuwait claimed royalties and taxes due; AMINOIL's liabilities to third parties as of 19 September 1977; and damages in relation to "lost oil" as a result of AMINOIL's failure to operate the oil fields efficiently and in accordance with the terms of the 1948 concession that provided for "good oil field practice."[24] AMINOIL claimed payments in respect of loss of profits; compensation; the value of the assets; and reimbursement for overpayment allegedly made by AMINOIL to the government.

Relevant legal issues:

- Applicable Law: *Lex Arbitri*: the tribunal found that article IV of the 1979 arbitration agreement made the proceedings subject to the mandatory provisions of French law as the law of the seat of arbitration. The agreement left to the tribunal the power to prescribe procedural rules, insofar as French law permitted, "on the basis of natural justice and principles of transnational arbitration."[25]

- Proper Law: The tribunal observed that the choice of law clause of the 1979 arbitral agreement stated: "the law governing the substantive issues between the Parties shall be determined by the Tribunal having regard to the quality of the Parties, the transnational character of their relations and the principles of law and practice prevailing in the modern world." The tribunal found that "Kuwait law applied to many matters over which it was the law most directly involved" and that public international law, relevant as well, was "part of the law of Kuwait."[26]

- Legality of the Nationalization: According to the tribunal, the decree was a valid exercise of the right of nationalization. The tribunal found that the nationalization was "neither confiscatory nor discriminatory." The tribunal concluded that the nationalization was not inconsistent with the concession.[27]

- Principles of Indemnification: According to the award, "appropriate compensation" under the terms of the General Assembly Resolution 1803 was to be determined depending on the circumstances of the case rather than on interpretation of terms such as "prompt, adequate and effective" or "fair." The tribunal held that compensation was to be assessed with regard to the legitimate expectations of the parties reflected in the "equilibrium" of the contract.[28]

Decision: The tribunal estimated royalties, taxes due to the Government of Kuwait and liabilities to third parties. The tribunal also assessed the value of AMINOIL's compensation. Both sums were offset, resulting in a balance in favor of AMINOIL, payable on July 1, 1982.[29]

Libyan American Oil Company (LIAMCO) vs. Government of the Libyan Arab Republic, 1977[30]

In 1955 the Libyan Ministry of Petroleum granted three concessions to the Libyan American Oil company (LIAMCO). Following the revolution in 1969, the new government of Libya negotiated changes in the economic provisions of the concessions. In September 1973, the Libyan Revolutionary Command Council promulgated a law nationalizing 51 percent of LIAMCO's concession rights. In February 1974, the remaining 49 percent of LIAMCO's rights were also nationalized. Although there were provisions in the law for compensation, no compensation was actually offered to LIAMCO.

Object of the claim: LIAMCO claimed that the nationalization laws constituted a breach of the concessions. In the event of LIAMCO not being restored to its concession rights, LIAMCO claimed damages or compensation.

Relevant legal issues:

- Applicable Law: The tribunal observed that "It is an accepted principle of international law that the arbitral rules of procedure shall be determined by the agreement of the parties, or in default of such agreement, by decision of the Arbitral Tribunal, independently of the local law of the seat of arbitration."[31] In this case, in the absence of a choice of law for the procedure, the tribunal determined that the principles contained in the Draft Convention on Arbitral Procedure elaborated by the International Law Commission of the United Nations in 1958 were to govern the procedure.
- Proper Law: According to the tribunal, the law governing the concessions was to be determined by reference to the general principles of international law, which provided that a contract was governed by the law expressly or impliedly chosen by the

parties. In the present case, the law chosen by the parties was Libyan law insofar as it was compatible with international law, and, in a subsidiary role, the general principles of law. The arbitrator found that, in general, Libyan law was in conformity with international law and the general principles of law.

- Legality of the Nationalization: The tribunal observed that the sovereign right of the state to nationalize was recognized in state practice and several General Assembly resolutions which reflected the dominant trend of international opinion in this respect. The tribunal also observed that nationalization is not unlawful as long as it is not discriminatory and is not accompanied by some other wrongful act. In the view of the arbitrator, international law no longer inquired into the motives for the nationalization to see if it involved a legitimate public purpose, unless those motives were discriminatory. The tribunal held that, in the case in question, the nationalization had not been discriminatory.

Decision: The arbitrator observed that "*restitutio in integrum* is generally impossible in international law."[32] The tribunal considered that restitutio amounted to an order to revoke nationalization measures which in the present case were not in themselves unlawful. The tribunal concluded that an award declaring that the nationalization laws were ineffective to transfer rights under the concessions would be contrary to the right to nationalize and were practically unenforceable. It was determined that the right for compensation existed and LIAMCO was entitled to it. The compensation was calculated by adding claim for value of plant and equipment, loss of concession, interest and costs.[33]

The decisions in the AMINOIL and Libyan nationalization cases have been published. Commenting on these and similar arbitration cases, Lord Wilberforce said at an International Law Association (ILA) meeting in 1981:

"Arbitration is now a huge industry—concerned with disputes between rich states and powerful multinationals ... This means that the people involved in this business are now the foremost lawyers ... The big brains. It means that they are making law—making it at the top level from which it will filter down to national domestic courts contrary to the traditional process of domestic to international."[34]

Professor Richard Bentham makes the following remarks on the contribution of the awards in those international arbitration cases to building a new lex mercatoria and to providing an appropriate framework for the resolution of disputes arising under petroleum agreements:

"Arbitration and the law developed from it are essential to maintain and foster world trade, and it is probably not an exaggeration to say that the decisions of arbitral tribunals are at present building a new lex mercatoria – a new law for international trade – a law which may help to resolve the continuing conflict between the concepts of *pacta sunt servanda* on the one hand and 'changing circumstances' on the other."[35]

The Abu Dhabi Experience: Certain Recent Developments

International arbitration has been adopted as a method of settling disputes in Abu Dhabi oil concessions as in other oil concessions throughout the Middle East. Since the original old-style concessions, through those granted in the period 1967–1971, up to and including the most recent concessions of 1980–1981, arbitration has been incorporated as a method for settling disputes, with certain changes being implemented in the drafting of the arbitration clauses of these successive agreements.

The text of Article 15 of the original oil concession of 1939 dealing with the settlement of disputes has already been quoted above. Reference has also been made to the Abu Dhabi arbitration case of 1951, which arose under the 1939 concession and which is, incidentally, the only oil arbitration case arising under a petroleum concession in which Abu Dhabi was involved. It is interesting in this context, for the sake of comparison, to refer to the way the arbitration clauses included in the most recent concession agreements of 1980–1981 were drafted. Here we take as an example, for illustrative purposes, the arbitration clause in one of the most recent of these agreements—the oil concession agreement with Deminex of May 3, 1981. Article 35 of this agreement deals with arbitration (the full text of this Article was quoted in Chapter 2 when reviewing the provisions of the Deminex Agreement).[36]

No concession agreements have been concluded in Abu Dhabi since 1982. We therefore do not know for sure how the arbitration clause would have been drafted in newer concession agreements. However, a most interesting development in the Abu Dhabi oil industry concerns the methods of dispute settlement reflected in certain recent agreements concluded between ADNOC and groups of oil companies operating in Abu Dhabi – including some of the majors – or separate companies. Although these are not in the form of concession agreements, some of them relate to joint venture arrangements and technical or management services, etc. A standard arbitration clause has been drafted and adopted, through discussions and mutual consent between the concerned parties, and inserted in the agreements referred to. This standard "arbitration clause" reads as follows:

> The Parties shall use their best efforts to settle all disputes or claims arising out of or in relation to this Agreement or any breach thereof. Should any difference or dispute of any kind arise between the Parties in connection with or arising out of this Agreement which cannot amicably be resolved within three hundred and sixty (360) days, then such difference or dispute shall be settled finally by arbitration in Abu Dhabi under the Procedural Rules of the Abu Dhabi Commercial Conciliation and Arbitration Center ("ADCCAC") by three (3) arbitrators, one to be nominated by each

party and the third to be agreed by the two nominated arbitrators and failing such agreement, the third arbitrator to be appointed by the Secretary General of ADCCAC from the international panel of arbitrators maintained by ADCCAC. All arbitration proceedings shall be in English and the award of the arbitrators shall be in accordance with the laws of Abu Dhabi and the United Arab Emirates. The award shall be final and binding upon both parties.[37]

When comparing this new arbitration clause with Article 35 of the Deminex Concession Agreement of 1981, one cannot fail to notice the important improvements introduced in the new clause concerning the procedural rules and regulations under which the arbitration is to be conducted, the venue of arbitration, the "appointing authority," or the applicable law. The adoption of this new arbitration clause in recent agreements between national companies and foreign partners reflects a radical change in the climate of the relationships between foreign oil companies and the host country (or its national company) and indicates confidence on the part of foreign oil companies in the local legal infrastructure and institutions of the host country.

7

Recent Developments in Relationships between the Government and Oil Companies

As long as oil and gas continue to play a crucial role in the economies and welfare of the countries of the world, be they producers, exporters or importers of petroleum, the study and analysis of the relationships between oil companies and their host governments will remain an important subject for students of petroleum and indeed for all those concerned with the various aspects of this dynamic and complex industry.

Both oil companies and host governments rely on each other and will continue to do so for the foreseeable future. They are both under pressure to make concerted efforts to meet energy challenges and to cater for the energy needs of the international community. Most host governments will require risk capital investment from the oil companies, in increasing amounts, as well as these companies' expertise, technology and secured market outlets. At the same time, the oil companies will continue to require new areas for their exploration and production activities to secure sufficient amounts of equity petroleum, and will continue to look for lucrative opportunities for the investment of their surplus funds and the full employment of their qualified technical and managerial staff.

This chapter will begin by providing a brief review of what some specialists in the field believe should form the basis of constructive and equitable relationships between oil companies and host governments. The second part of this chapter will review and examine some of the recent developments in the Abu Dhabi oil industry and show how the general framework of the oil industry in Abu Dhabi might accommodate these developments.

The Evolving Relationships between Oil Companies and Host Governments

One writer who has taken a special interest in the subject of the evolving relationships between oil companies and host governments is Dr. Alfred Boulos, who was for many years one of the senior officials of CONOCO Inc. and who is now working as an oil consultant through the consultancy firm Boulos International. In a conference organized by the Emirates Center for Strategic Studies and Research (ECSSR) in Abu Dhabi (October 1996), Dr. Boulos presented a paper entitled: "The Past and Present Contractual Make-up: Options for Negotiating Future Concessions."

The main purpose of Dr. Boulos' paper, as its title indicates, was to present the author's insight and recommendations concerning the options for negotiating future oil concessions between host governments and foreign oil companies.

In the first part of his paper, Dr. Boulos provided a thorough review of the historical developments in the international oil industry and in the relationships between host countries and oil companies, particularly the significant period of 1970–1973. In the second part of his paper, Dr. Boulos outlines his conclusions and recommendations concerning the principles which should guide the negotiation of future oil agreements, in light of the lessons drawn from historical developments. He begins his conclusions by highlighting "the new emphasis on common objectives between

[142]

host governments and energy companies" and "the mutuality of interests" between the two parties:

> We need to emphasize that the common objectives of both the energy company and the host government are similar. The primary goal of the company in the joint venture is to create wealth in the form of discovery of petroleum. Likewise, the primary goal of the host government in the joint venture is to create wealth, in the form of economic growth, to benefit its people. Reasonable and equitable considerations should ensure that the finite amount of wealth created can be fairly provided for both the company and government.
>
> ... A new contractual make-up based on common objectives and mutuality of interests provides the appropriate foundation for future options for negotiation success. Such new contractual make-up brings a positive atmosphere to the discussions. It allays suspicions. It increases the basis for sincere efforts by both parties to succeed in a joint venture agreement even in the face of serious differences of opinion. In every way, this doctrine of mutuality of interests is the key to success in a joint venture.[1]

This doctrine of "mutuality of interests" between host governments and oil companies seems to be a favorite thesis for Dr. Boulos. In 1990 he had submitted a paper entitled: "Mutuality of Interests Between Companies and Governments—Myth or Fact?" to the International Bar Association's (IBA) Energy Law Seminar held in the Netherlands in April 1990.

It is interesting to note that the most eloquent critic of Dr. Boulos' thesis did not come from a producing country in this region, or from a developing country, but from a western oil producing country: Canada. The outspoken opponent was the Honorable Marc Lalonde, former Canadian Minister of Energy. He presented at that seminar a paper entitled "Energy Companies and their Host Governments: To Each his Own." The paper expressed a clear disagreement with – and a reasoned criticism of – Dr. Boulos' main thesis of "mutuality of interests" and advanced a different view on the nature of the relationship between host governments and oil companies. In order to provide the reader with a different view of the relationship between governments and oil companies, it is appropriate to cite extracts from Mr. Lalonde's paper. One must remember, however, that it is only natural for a representative of a host government, like Mr. Lalonde, to have a view on this topic which differs from the view expressed by Dr. Boulos—who has held several positions in oil companies. Each one will view the subject from a different angle. As stated by Mr. Lalonde: "For each of us, our view of the world is framed by our own past experience." Lalonde begins by saying:

> The occasional convergence of interests between international oil companies and host governments on the occasion of successful negotiations does not allow such a process to be elevated into a so-called doctrine of mutuality of interests.
>
> ... The overall goal as well as the general and the specific objectives of governments are much broader than those of international oil companies; they are of a different order and governments should, and will, resist attempts to bring them to the same level. In particular, energy issues cannot be seen in isolation any more; they involve many aspects of government policies, be they fiscal or environmental, and this trend is bound to grow.
>
> ... The goal of governments is of a very different nature. It is to promote and protect the collective and individual well being of its citizens. The creation of wealth through economic growth should be a major goal of governments but it is by no means their exclusive or even their primary goal; and certainly not only through the development of hydrocarbon resources. There are other competing and equally important goals such as the collective security of the nation, the protection of weaker elements in society, the maintenance of decent public services, etc. The current debate in Western countries around 'sustainable growth' is merely another example of the establishment of priorities that conflict with the principle of maximization of wealth and economic growth.[2]

Lalonde indicates that if the goals of governments and oil companies differ, so too do their objectives when it comes to the development of hydrocarbons. In conclusion, Mr. Lalonde makes the following statement:

> Nowadays, issues of foreign policy, environment, regional development, taxation, are only a few of those that have a bearing on energy policy. And I suspect that these interrelationships will increase rather than diminish in the future. It is most important for energy companies to recognize and adjust to such an evolution. That evolution should be seen as further evidence that the priorities and objectives of host governments are not of the same order as those of the international companies.
>
> This does not mean that these priorities and objectives are incompatible. The task of reconciling them, if possible, is the responsibility of able and conscientious negotiators for companies and for governments. To elevate this process ... to a doctrine of mutuality of interests does not appear to me, however, to be the right analysis. I do not believe in benevolent international oil companies. I do not say that they are malevolent. I am only saying that both companies and governments should be guided by their enlightened self-interest. The deal they may thus strike is more likely to be respected by future governments, than if it is perceived as having been the result of some cozy mutual interest negotiations.
>
> The issue of what is the national interest is one for national governments alone to decide, not one dependent on a 'partnership' with international oil companies; the issue of the international common good in the energy field may be a question of partnership, but one between the governments of consuming and producing countries, not between the governments of producing countries and international oil companies.[3]

The author agrees whole-heartedly that confrontation between governments and companies should not be the basis on which workable relationships should be founded; and that cooperation is necessary and profitable for both. Furthermore, the author emphasizes the view that:

> There are undoubtedly legitimate interests for both the government concerned and the oil company, and prudence and flexibility dictate that a compromise should be sought to attain a reasonable equilibrium between these interests upon the conclusion of petroleum arrangements or when the government sets out the legal framework for these arrangements. The properly conducted negotiation between the parties based on proper appreciation of the legitimate interests of each party would lead to a balanced and reasonable reconciliation of these interests.[4]

One way to contribute to the study of this subject would be to refer to the experience of a large, old producer – as has been done in this book – in order to see how this reconciliation of the legitimate interests has been effectively achieved and how smooth and rewarding relationships can be successfully established on cooperation between a host government and foreign oil companies. In particular one might cite the way the participation agreements between the government of Abu Dhabi and the old concessionaries were implemented and how a host government participated, through its national oil company, with foreign oil companies in the development of its petroleum resources in a satisfactory and mutually beneficial manner over a long period.

One may refer back to Chapter 3, which explores the practical modalities of the implementation of the participation arrangements in Abu Dhabi and the pattern of relationships established between the national partner and foreign companies within the operating companies (ADCO and ADMA-OPCO) which were established under those arrangements. If these successful arrangements within the framework of the participation agreements were introduced in already existing concessions, nothing prevents the adoption of similar principles and arrangements in new agreements to be concluded either with the same or with new parties.

In conclusion, both parties to the contractual relationship (the host government and the oil company) have legitimate interests to protect.

A prudent government should not overlook the legitimate interests of the oil companies with which it will enter into agreement. By the same token, oil companies would be well advised to refrain from taking advantage of their superior bargaining position in the early stages – due to the lack of knowledge in the country concerned about its petroleum potential and its desperate need for their expertise and capabilities – to secure one-sided, onerous and rigid terms and conditions. Undoubtedly, the existence of such conditions is bound to breed discontent and inequity in the country concerned. Later, when oil has been discovered in commercial quantities, the prices of oil go up and the relative bargaining position shifts in favor of the host country. This will inevitably lead to persistent requests by the country concerned to modify the terms of the initial arrangements to make them equitable by negotiation, if possible, and ultimately, by unilateral action in the event that the oil companies delay or do not respond favorably to the request for change.

The best way to curb the need for such unilateral actions and to maintain smooth, long term relations is by making the contents of the petroleum legal framework equitable from the start in recognizing the legitimate interests of both parties. Since "prevention is better than cure," the parties should also anticipate the possible need for certain future changes and stipulate suitable provisions to bring about such changes in an orderly fashion in order to maintain a reasonable balance between the legitimate interests of both parties.

Recent Developments in the Abu Dhabi Oil Industry

Environmental Regulations

It is well known that most of the old-style oil concession agreements concluded in the Middle East did not take into account matters related to environmental protection in oil exploration and production operations. The original oil concession agreements concluded by the government of Abu Dhabi (in 1939 for onshore areas and in 1953 for offshore areas) were no exception and contained no provisions concerning environmental protection or resource conservation. This situation did not improve significantly under the set of concessions granted by Abu Dhabi in the period 1967–71, except for the introduction of an article entitled "Diligent and Workmanlike Operations," which contains a reference, in broad terms, to the reasonable precautions that oil companies should take when conducting their petroleum operations. The article reads:

(a) The Company shall conduct its operations in the Concession Area with diligence and in a workmanlike manner and in accordance with accepted methods and standards of the petroleum industry.

(b) The Company shall take all reasonable precautions against fire and any unwarranted wasting of crude oil, natural gas or water.[5]

When an oil company's concession covers offshore operations, another paragraph is added to this article, according to which the company should undertake to "take adequate precautions for the protection of navigation, fishing and pearling and that they will comply with all reasonable requirements of the competent authorities affecting the navigation of ships and aircraft and the prevention of pollution of the seas by oil."[6]

The most recent oil concession agreements, concluded in the period 1980–81, did not introduce any improvements in terms of environmental protection, and only contain the "Diligent and Workmanlike Operations," provision, identical to that cited above. Therefore, we can conclude that, in general, oil concession agreements concluded by Abu Dhabi, including the most recent concessions of 1980–81, made no specific reference to environmental protection. Under those concessions, the operating companies were under no real obligation to protect the environment—neither precautionary nor substantive preventive measures were required.

In 1978, the Abu Dhabi government promulgated the Law on the Conservation of Petroleum Resources. This law closely follows a model established by OPEC for adoption in member countries. It stipulates rules and regulations according to which all operations (exploration, drilling, production, etc.) should be carried out to comply with the most efficient scientific techniques and methods. It spells out, inter alia, the precautions that should be taken to safeguard the health and safety of employees and to prevent pollution, as well as the obligations of the operating companies to report to government authorities and gain prior authorizations and permissions. The utilization of gas is regulated and the law imposes fines for violations of its provisions.

This law contains only one article referring in broad terms to environmental protection – Article 56 – which reads as follows:

> The operator shall take all the necessary precautions to prevent pollution of the air, underground and surface waters, territorial waters, and waters of the continental shelf, shores, and all islands within the territorial waters and the continental shelf. If the operator's operations cause pollution, the operator shall immediately eliminate the resulting effects in accordance with modern techniques. The quantity and quality of the operator's devices and materials required for handling pollution shall be commensurate with the size of the operator's operations and subject to the Abu Dhabi Petroleum Department's written approval.[7]

In view of the increased global awareness of environmental issues, environmental protection and sustainable development, which have become some of the most important global concerns of this era, both the federal government of the UAE and the government of the emirate of Abu Dhabi have promulgated legislation in this respect. At the federal level, Federal Law No. 7 (the Federal Environmental Law) was promulgated in 1993. This law relates to the creation of the Federal Environmental Agency and sets out the objectives of this body, its management and administration (the composition of its Board, its functions and working procedures, voting and decision making), financial affairs and sources of income. It does not contain any provisions concerning the regime governing the control of the environment, or any related to the substance of regulations or measures concerning environmental protection. However, a modern, comprehensive Federal Law on Environment Protection and Development has subsequently been promulgated. The petroleum industry has, of course, its own environmental concerns and cannot neglect issues related to environment protection and the conservation of resources. The oil industry of Abu Dhabi is no exception. Prompted by its awareness of environmental concerns in the different phases of its oil operations and by its interests regarding the sustainable development of the petroleum resources of Abu Dhabi, ADNOC took the initiative to prepare, adopt and implement an efficacious and comprehensive Health, Safety and Environment Management System (HSEMS) for the oil industry of Abu Dhabi. ADNOC felt that in order for the HSEMS to be effective it had to apply to the whole oil industry in Abu Dhabi. In the words of ADNOC's management: "Many commendable initiatives have been undertaken to better control some individual HSE costs and issue drivers in each Directorate (of ADNOC) or Group Company. We must now take a look at all our processes and develop integrated management solutions."[8] Furthermore, the management states: "ADNOC believes it to be in the best interest of the Directorates and Group Companies to have a comprehensive policy and guidelines for Health, Safety and Environment programs. ADNOC further believes that by working together, each of the Directorates and Group Companies will have a stronger, more efficient and cost effective program."[9]

For that purpose, ADNOC established a Group HSE Committee composed of representatives from ADNOC, its wholly owned affiliates and the oil companies operating in Abu Dhabi with which it participates, as well as foreign oil companies, including some of the majors. These companies are collectively referred to in Abu Dhabi as the ADNOC Group Companies.

A document incorporating the HSEMS and entitled "ADNOC: Health, Safety and Environment Management System (HSEMS)" was circulated by ADNOC in 1997. In this document, under the title "HSEMS Development & Application Guidelines" it states that:

> These Guidelines have been styled by the ADNOC Group HSE Committee after those proposed by the E&P Forum [The Oil Industry International Exploration & Production Forum, which brings together a number of international oil companies]. The E&P Forum Safety, Health and Personnel Competence and Environmental Quality Committee formed a special ad hoc HSEMS task force to develop these guidelines. This same basic structure has been adopted by the International Standards Organization for the Environmental Management System (EMS) Standard Series 1400 (ISO 14000) and was used for the ISO 9000 standard services setting forth the Safety Management System (SMS).[10]

The HSEMS Document provides a brief summary of the wide and comprehensive range of subjects covered by the System:

> This HSE Management System includes a description of roles and responsibilities for implementing and maintaining the system (Section 3.3), procedures for establishing HSE objectives and targets (Section 3.4) and for implementing HSE programs (Section 3.5). After the initial implementation of the HSEMS, ADNOC's goal is to establish a continuous improvement process to ensure that the HSEMS will be an integral part of each business (Section 3.6). The HSEMS includes HSE audit (Section 3.7) and management review (Section 3.8) procedures. Finally, the success of the HSEMS depends on there being clear, two-way communications and information exchange among and between all levels of the ADNOC Directorates and Group Companies organizations (Section 3.9).[11]

This study will not review the contents of this comprehensive system. The aim is simply to show that the Abu Dhabi oil industry is now committed to implementing a modern and efficacious environmental protection system of international standard and that the oil companies operating in Abu Dhabi, which have among their shareholders some of the major international oil companies, cooperated willingly in the preparation and implementation of an advanced environmental protection system, although they are under no such specific obligation in accordance with their concession agreements or other contractual arrangements with the Abu Dhabi government. This demonstrates that the arrangements now in effect between the foreign oil companies and the government of Abu Dhabi can accommodate reasonable developments and cope with changes which may take place in the circumstances surrounding oil operations. Furthermore, this illustrates the fact that dialogue and cooperation between oil companies and host countries can produce gratifying results to preserve the evolving relationships between the two parties.

Appointment of Nationals as General Managers of Joint Operating Companies (JOCs)

In the mid-1990s ADNOC adopted a new position regarding the appointment of General Managers among the operating companies in which ADNOC retains a shareholding percentage along with other foreign oil companies. The consistent practice in this regard, since the time when these companies were established and until the mid-1990s, had been to appoint a secondee of one of the foreign shareholding companies as General Manager of the joint operating company (while, in certain cases, a national was appointed to the post of Assistant or Deputy General Manager). However, ADNOC adopted a new position in the mid-1990s, requiring the appointment of a national as General Manager of some of the operating companies, including GASCO and ADGAS.

Abu Dhabi Gas Industries Limited (GASCO)

GASCO is controlled by ADNOC (which holds 68 percent of the equity capital) in association with Total and Shell (15 percent each) and Partex (2 percent). Concerning the administration of GASCO, according to Article 7.04(11) of the Joint Venture Agreement, "The General Manager shall be nominated by ADNOC and be appointed by the Board on terms and conditions approved by the Board ..."[12]

Until the mid-1990s, the appointment of a General Manager to GASCO required the unanimous agreement of ADNOC and the other shareholders to appoint, alternately, a recommended secondee of Shell or Total. In late 1995, ADNOC decided to nominate, for the first time, a national as General Manager of GASCO, with effect from January 1996, and the Board approved the appointment of the ADNOC nominee.

Abu Dhabi Gas Liquefaction Company Ltd. (ADGAS)

ADGAS processes and exports LNG, LPG and Pentane Plus from its plant on Das Island, situated 160 km northwest of Abu Dhabi city. It was reincorporated in Abu Dhabi in 1977 to acquire the entire assets of an identically named company which had been incorporated in Bermuda in 1972. According to Law No. 2 of 1977 establishing ADGAS, the equity capital of the company was originally divided as follows: ADNOC, 51 percent; BP, 16.33 percent; Total, 8.17 percent; and Mitsui Group, 24.5 percent. Concerning the appointment of a General Manager, Article 7.05 of the Participants Agreement (of 1977 between ADNOC, BP, Total and Mitsui) stipulates that the General Manager should be "appointed by the Board of Directors, upon nomination by ADNOC, which [sic] nomination shall be made after consultation with the other shareholders." In practice, since its reincorporation in

1977 and until 1997, the General Manager of ADGAS had been, alternately, a BP or a Total secondee.

In December 1997, however, it was agreed between ADNOC and the other shareholders of ADGAS to increase ADNOC's shareholding to 70 percent, which resulted in the present shareholding of ADGAS: ADNOC, 70 percent; Mitsui, 15 percent; BP, 10 percent; and Total, 5 percent. This radical change was achieved through a combination of negotiations between ADNOC and its partners, and was a result of mutual consent rather than unilateral action by ADNOC.

Concerning the appointment of the General Manager, Article 7.05 of the Restated Participants Agreement, concluded in December 1997, maintained almost the same wording as the article in the original Participants Agreement of 1977, to the effect that the General Manager of ADGAS should be appointed by the Board of Directors upon nomination by ADNOC after consultation with the other participants. However, ADNOC thought it now appropriate to nominate to the post of General Manager of ADGAS a national of the UAE rather than a recommended secondee from the foreign shareholders, as had been the practice ever since the establishment of ADGAS. The Board of Directors of ADGAS endorsed this nomination and approved the appointment of the ADNOC national nominee.

The process of replacing the foreign general managers of the joint operating companies (JOCs) has continued. Presently, almost all the general managers of the JOCs are nationals. These developments concerning the shareholding percentages and management of ADGAS provide an example of how the legitimate interests of a national company can be secured through mutual agreement rather than a unilateral act of the host country.

The developments referred to in this chapter, which came about as a result of negotiations based on mutual understanding and consent, demonstrate that the contractual arrangements now in effect between the host (Abu Dhabi) and the operating oil companies can accommodate new changes in circumstances and cope with the reasonable requirements of the host while preserving the basic characteristics of the arrangements and the continuity of smooth relations.

8

Future Objectives
of Abu Dhabi Petroleum Policy

W hen ADNOC obtained exclusive permits over five blocks in 1980, it deduced that all large and most medium-sized hydrocarbon accumulations had probably already been detected, but felt it was imperative to use state-of-the-art technology to locate complementary medium and small fields. It was also decided that ADNOC and its upstream affiliates would adopt and carry out exploration programs to add to Abu Dhabi's knowledge of its oil geology and acquire more data about known reservoirs and structures. In other words, Abu Dhabi realized that it had an interest in continuing exploration activities in those areas not adequately explored and in carrying out further appraisals of existing reservoirs and structures, although the development of any new capacity discovered might not be immediate.

Building up Production Capacity

Abu Dhabi has set itself the objective of stepping up its total oil production capacity from 2.85–3 mbpd in 2006 to 3.7 mbpd in 2010. ADNOC's upstream subsidiaries (ADCO, ADMA and ZADCO) are contributing to this expansion in the following ways:

- ZADCO, which operates the Upper Zakum field (considered to be the largest oil field in Abu Dhabi with estimated recoverable reserves of sixteen to twenty billion barrels), is presently carrying out an important secondary development program (based on the use of extensive water injection) that is designed to increase the production capacity of the field from 550,000 bpd to 750,000 bpd. When ADNOC decided in April 2005 to sell 28 percent of its interests in the Upper Zakum field to Exxon Mobil, it was in order to gain access to the advanced technology required for increasing the recovery rate at the field, which suffers from low reservoir pressure.

- ADMA is planning to increase the sustainable capacity of the Umm Shaif and Lower Zakum fields from the 460,000 bpd reached in 2002 to 600,000 bpd.
- ADCO is also planning to step up its production capacity from 1.2 mbpd to 1.4 mbpd. New field development is currently underway at the Al-Dabbiya and Al-Rumaitha fields in the northeast Bab area, which was due to be completed in 2006. Thus far, however, there are no reports to confirm that this has been achieved.

Abu Dhabi may be pursuing this strategy to develop the maximum possible production capacity in order to be in a position to use it whenever market conditions allow the export of larger volumes of oil. As Abu Dhabi is characterized by low population and large reserves, its primary concern is control over production in the short term, and an orderly and efficient development of its resources in the long term.

Aside from the associated gas produced in the onshore and offshore oil fields, Abu Dhabi has large reserves of unassociated natural gas. As mentioned in Chapter 4, ADNOC's aim is to develop natural gas reservoirs and to boost non-associated gas production from both onshore and offshore structures in such a way as to ensure a stable supply of gas to local users and to export-oriented projects.

Gas consumption has been growing rapidly in the UAE and will continue to rise. The initial phase of the gas distribution network in the cities of Abu Dhabi and Al Ain, which ADNOC Distribution has started installing, is scheduled for completion in 2008. This gas network, which is bound to witness continuous expansion in the coming years, will certainly lead to the growth of natural gas as a domestic energy source. This is set to be one of the future trends in the field of energy consumption in Abu Dhabi. In this context, Abu Dhabi has reason to be proud of its promotion of the Dolphin Project as an important example of a regional project in the field of gas, characterized by cooperation between the UAE (Abu Dhabi and Dubai), Qatar, Oman and possibly even Pakistan at a later stage. It is hoped that this project will herald an era of increasing utilization of gas as a source of energy and of beneficial regional cooperation in this field.

ADNOC Distribution is also promoting the use of compressed natural gas (CNG) as a motor fuel; in 2005 ADNOC Distribution opened its first pilot filling station for vehicles running on CNG. If there is sufficient demand and the operation proves profitable, ADNOC plans to build more CNG filling stations. Furthermore, in conjunction with two other subsidiaries (ADMA and ADGAS), ADNOC began to promote the use of CNG in April 2004 when it launched a project to substitute liquid fuel with CNG in motor vehicles circulating on Das Island. This substitution process was subsequently completed in the same year.[1]

An extensive acreage of Abu Dhabi is not covered by petroleum permits, having been relinquished by the former concessionaires. Certain blocks of this acreage could be granted to ADNOC, in addition to the five exclusive prospecting licenses it presently holds. Some of this open acreage will probably remain available in the future to those foreign oil companies that have the financial and technical capability to sustain a reasonable exploration and development effort in Abu Dhabi.

In terms of the main principles that continue to guide the oil policy of Abu Dhabi, the emirate believes that the development of its petroleum industry is best served by allowing foreign oil companies to play a direct role in the industry. Furthermore, Abu Dhabi has a long history of reasonably good relations with foreign oil companies operating in the country. Therefore, any real change in this policy in the few coming years or any departure from its basic elements is unlikely. To be more specific:

• Abu Dhabi has been generally satisfied with the participation agreements with the oil companies presently covering the main fields. In the normal course of events one would not expect any change in the framework of these relationships.

• As for the smaller companies operating under concession agreements with no government involvement, no imminent change is expected here either. Four of these companies are presently producers. According to these agreements the government has the option to participate upon commercial discovery of oil. The only change one might foresee in the status of these companies is if the government, under certain circumstances in the future, decides to acquire greater control of the oil industry. In such circumstances it may exercise its participation option in some of these concessions.

Chapter 3 outlined the role played by ADNOC in the oil industry of Abu Dhabi and stated that the organizational structure of the industry is built around ADNOC. Therefore, in order to construct a picture of the future of the Abu Dhabi oil industry one should examine the future role of ADNOC. Based on established facts, objectives and trends, as well as past experience, the future role of ADNOC in the next few years can be outlined as follows:

The Future Role of ADNOC

ADNOC will work towards consolidating its present position rather than pursuing a path of quick expansion. In the field of human resources it will concentrate its efforts on developing a highly qualified staff to cope with its multifarious expansion.

The exploration programs adopted and being carried out by ADNOC directly or through its subsidiaries in order to assess the oil potential and capabilities of the country will continue in the coming years. In the field of production ADNOC's share will increase: first, through increases in the level of production of the major operating companies (ADCO and ADMA) after the completion of the development projects currently being implemented (within the limits of the allowable production ceilings dictated by petroleum policy); and second, through the production of the other fields which are being developed outside the scope of the major concessions.

Abu Dhabi is committed to increasing its production capacity, with ambitious plans to gradually step up total production capacity to 3.7 mbpd by 2010. With those quantities of oil at its disposal, ADNOC's international marketing activities will certainly increase. It is expected that most of the national oil companies in the exporting countries will follow a similar path, thus playing a much more significant role in the international oil market at the expense of the international majors.

Abu Dhabi has extensive proven reserves of non-associated natural gas. This study referred earlier to the important projects being implemented by ADNOC and its affiliates for intensive development of associated and non-associated gas. ADNOC will also be involved in the gas industry through its gas distribution network, which will lead to a gradual increase in the utilization of natural gas as a domestic energy source. Furthermore, ADNOC is promoting the use of compressed natural gas (CNG) as a domestic motor fuel.

In the field of refining, it is significant that in 2000 ADNOC's wholly-owned affiliate, TAKREER (which oversees refining operations) installed two 140,000 bpd condensate splitter trains at Ruwais refinery, raising its refining capacity to 420,000 bpd; increasing Abu Dhabi's total refining capacity from the Ruwais and Umm Al Nar refineries to 508,000 bpd (420,000 bpd from Ruwais and 88,000 bpd from Umm Al Nar).[2] It is likely that this trend of increasing refining capacity oriented for export will continue in the future.

In this respect, ADNOC will follow the prevailing objective of OPEC and OAPEC to work towards increasing the minimal share of the oil-producing countries in the world's refining capacity and other downstream operations.

ADNOC was late to enter the petrochemicals field; its first petrochemical project – Abu Dhabi Polymers Company Ltd. (Borouge) – did not begin production until December 2001 but it is significant that Borouge (60 percent of which is owned by ADNOC) proved to be quite dynamic and started at this early stage of its career to implement expansion plans. In April 2005 the company completed a second phase of development which increased its initial capacity by around 30 percent. After a third phase of development, which was provisionally scheduled for completion in 2007, Borouge plans to further boost its capacity. Therefore, ADNOC can be expected to become more involved in petrochemicals operations in the coming few years.

In terms of investment abroad, certain commercial aims (to lend a degree of flexibility to the company's operations; diversify fields of lucrative investment; consolidate the company's position in the market; and secure access to the industrialization process) and political objectives of the state (to strengthen relations and cooperation with friendly nations) have led ADNOC to make select investments abroad, like some other national oil companies in the region. In 1984, ADNOC formed a joint venture with Abu Dhabi

Investment Authority (ADIA) to invest in petroleum operations overseas. The joint venture company, called the International Petroleum Investment Company (IPIC), has already concluded a number of deals with international parties and is planning to further expand its activities.

ADNOC has proved that it is capable of taking positive initiatives, is open to new concepts and technological innovations and has introduced many changes in its different operations and activities. ADNOC can be expected to continue making successive improvements to its operations and to successfully ride the new trends in the oil industry.

Future Exploration and Exploitation Permits

Should the government decide to invite foreign oil companies to apply for exploration and exploitation permits covering parts of the relinquished areas, what legal framework might be adopted? In order to facilitate a comparison between the different forms of exploration and exploitation agreements, the following is a brief description of the main types of agreement that might be considered:

Modernized Concessions

In Chapter 2 the Deminex concession agreement concluded on May 3, 1981 was chosen to illustrate the latest model of concession agreement (modernized concession) adopted in Abu Dhabi. The most relevant provisions of that agreement were outlined in that chapter and, to avoid repetition, we refer the reader to the relevant sections of Chapter 2.

Production-Sharing Agreements (PSAs)

The main difference between concession regimes and contractual arrangements such as production-sharing agreements is that under concession regimes the host country grants the rights to explore and produce to oil companies (usually international), while under a production-sharing formula the host country keeps for itself (usually through its national oil company) the exclusive right to explore and produce, while the national oil company enters into subcontracts with oil companies for exploration and production. The international oil companies are, therefore, granted the status of risk-taking contractors, entitled to the reimbursement of their costs should commercial production begin, as well as a share of the production to remunerate their efforts. Moreover, while under concessions the government's take consists of taxes and royalties, under a production-sharing agreement the government's revenue is largely derived from its share of the oil produced. The production-sharing agreement stresses the element of control left with the state, using language confirming that the host country retains and is responsible for the management of operations. The basic features of the production-sharing approach are as follows:

- The foreign oil company is appointed by the host country as a "contractor" for a certain area. The contractor operates at its sole risk and expense under the control of the national oil company. It bears the risk of explorations. Therefore, if there is no commercial discovery, the loss is borne by the contractor.

- The foreign company is entitled to recovery of its costs out of the production from the contractual area at a stipulated rate equal to a percentage of production (usually between 25 and 40 percent).

- After cost recovery, the balance of production (called "profit oil") is shared on a pre-determined percentage split between the host country and the foreign oil company. There are several systems for splitting production. There can be a sole profit-oil split (85 percent to the host country and 15 percent to the foreign oil company, which does not pay income tax), or a progressive split based on one of two scales: Daily production according to a given scale: 60 percent of the production to the government and 40 percent to the foreign company if the production reaches 20,000 bpd; or, if the rate of production is between 20,000 bpd and 40,000 bpd, the government share will go up to 65 percent, leaving 35 percent for the company; and should the production rate reach between 40,000 and 60,000 bpd the government's share will go up to 70 percent leaving 30 percent for the oil company. Alternatively, the production split is based on the profitability of operations—when the realized profits from the operations go up, the share of the government in the production will go up; while if the profits are low the government share goes down and the company's share goes up to compensate for the low profits generated by the operations.

- As for the control and management of operations, under the PSA the concept of joint control of operations is adopted through a joint advisory committee (or a Joint Management Committee—JMC) that discusses and approves programs and budgets.

- As is the case in modern concessions and joint ventures, production-sharing contracts usually include requirements for specified work programs, periodic relinquishment of part of the original contract area, and termination of the agreement if no oil is found within a specified period.

Joint Ventures

The term "joint venture" as a specific form of exploration and production arrangement usually denotes a situation where the government of the host country grants, through a joint undertaking between the national company and a foreign company, exclusive rights to explore and produce petroleum, instead of granting these exclusive rights to a foreign concessionaire as in the old-style concession agreements. The main features of a typical joint venture are as follows:

- The costs and risks of the exploration phase are borne by the foreign oil company, and the host government contributes to costs only after a commercial discovery has been made.

- A joint venture will generally terminate if a commercial deposit of petroleum is not discovered by the end of the exploration period.

- The national oil company will normally reimburse its pro rata share of the exploration cost when the discovery has been made. In the production phase the host government (or its national oil company) will typically pay its share of operating costs and capital expenses.

With regard to the organization of the joint venture it is, broadly speaking, possible to distinguish three varieties:

The first is characterized by the formation of a separate legal entity owned by the host government (or its national oil company) and the oil company that makes the discovery. This entity is entrusted with the job of producing and sometimes marketing petroleum produced under the agreement. It pays royalties and tax to the relevant authorities, and net profits are shared according to each party's equity in the enterprise.

A second form of joint venture does not call for the formation of a separate legal entity jointly owned by the host government and the oil company, although actual operations are frequently controlled by a management committee consisting of representatives of both parties. Instead, by virtue of contractual arrangements, each party has a direct undivided interest in the exploitation area and in all oil produced from it. No new taxable entity is created and each party is liable for the payment of its royalty and tax.

The third approach (which has been used in Abu Dhabi) is the formation of a non-profit-making joint operating company (like ADCO or ADMA-OPCO) which is entrusted with the responsibility of carrying out all development and production operations at cost. The funds required are provided by the foreign oil company (or companies) and the national oil company. The newly created joint company does not market the production but rather delivers the oil to the shareholders in accordance with the joint venture agreement.

Normally, all important decisions in any form of joint venture must be submitted for the approval of the parties through certain mechanisms provided for in the agreement (such as a JMC). A sole risk clause is also included.

Service Agreements and Risk–Service Agreements

As their names indicate, these agreements are service contracts under which a host country (or its national oil company) hires the services of a foreign oil company which assumes the legal status of a "contractor." In case of commercial production in the contracting area, the foreign oil company is reimbursed for its costs and investments and paid for its services. However, although this is a service contract, the financial risk during the exploration phase and until commercial discovery is still borne by the contractor. The legal consequences attached to this type of agreement are that the foreign oil company is granted no mining or mineral rights and that the production belongs, in its entirety, to the host country or its national oil company. The foreign company, as contractor, only receives remuneration for its services.

Risk-service agreements are similar in their principles to production-sharing agreements and present similar features. The main difference lies in the mechanism for the recovery of costs and the remuneration paid to the contractor. Initially, and still in most cases, cost recovery and remuneration are made according to a mutually agreed formula and payments are made in cash (for instance at the rate of a certain sum per barrel produced). However, in some modern risk-service agreements the contractor receives oil in lieu of cash which brings the service agreement closer to the production-sharing agreement.

The basic differences between these regimes are of a legal nature and are of political significance. While from a legal standpoint the difference is fundamental, from an economic point of view, the difference lies more in the mechanism used to distribute the production and income arising from the arrangement. Under the concession system, with its varieties (including joint ventures), the government's take consists of taxes and royalties, and under production-sharing type agreements the government's revenue largely comes from its share of oil produced. The economics can be standardized by properly tailoring the terms of the arrangement through negotiations. This means that Abu Dhabi can opt to conclude any one of these types of agreement provided the basic terms and conditions are carefully prepared, drafted, negotiated and concluded.

Conclusion

It is likely that the government of Abu Dhabi will decide to retain the form of "modernized concession" entered into during the period 1980–1981 for a number of reasons, but in particular because this form of concession has been used in the emirate for many years and hence is familiar to both government officials and the concerned staff. However, if Abu Dhabi is to continue to use this form of concession, a number of refinements in the drafting and some specific improvements could be made concerning certain aspects of the text (for instance, the provisions related to arbitration and applicable law). Progress should continue whenever possible. The government may, however, adopt a different legal format for any new oil agreements it concludes, such as the production-sharing format. This format has many attractions for producing countries, which explains its popularity and widespread adoption both within and outside OPEC, including some countries in the region (Qatar, Egypt, Syria).

ADNOC may eventually decide to invite foreign oil companies to cooperate with it in further exploration and/or development in parts of the five blocks covered by its prospecting licenses. In that case, ADNOC will have to choose the appropriate legal framework to govern this cooperation. Should the Abu Dhabi government or ADNOC adopt the production-sharing form of agreement or a form of service contract as the legal framework of agreements, Abu Dhabi would become an ideal environment for experimentation and comparative analysis of different and distinct petroleum legal frameworks (including concessions agreements free of government involvement, participation arrangements, production-sharing agreements and service contracts) co-existing and competing with each other in the same arena.

Whatever the form of legal framework adopted in any new agreement to be concluded by Abu Dhabi, an appropriate financial package must be designed carefully and realistically for each individual situation, taking into account the characteristics of the area offered and the general conditions prevailing in the oil industry. An ideal formula would be to design the contractual terms for the oil companies in such a way that offered conditions are satisfactory both for large as well as small discoveries and that they safeguard the economic long-term interests of the host country and the oil company. Flexibility and progression are of the essence, while inflexibility and rigidity are undesirable. If the government's take is too high it could discourage the investor; if it is initially too low – in order to attract the oil company – when a commercial discovery is made it could create ill-feeling in the host country and tension in the relationship with the foreign company.

One possible approach to fiscal efficiency with an element of flexibility would consist of a sliding-scale fiscal package, which directly reflects costs such as that used in the modernized concessions concluded by Abu Dhabi in the early 1980s. In a production-sharing contract, this approach allows for the allocation to the foreign partner of a higher share of production for smaller production levels, deeper water, etc.

It seems that more flexibility and progressiveness will be needed in new agreements, given the expected instability in oil prices over the medium term. One approach would be to adopt fiscal terms that are directly linked to changes in oil prices. For example, in a production-sharing agreement, as the crude price drops, the contractor's share rises; as the prices go up the production share of the host country rises and the contractor's drops. Another approach to cope with the expected instability in oil prices would be to introduce terms which are linked to the rate of return achieved by the oil companies.

All these approaches are worthy of careful study and refinement of the mechanisms of their implementation in order to achieve greater flexibility, in contractual terms, which would allow for adaptation to changes in oil prices or in the oil company's rate of return without the need for major renegotiations. Efficient, pre-designed adaptation of certain contractual terms to changes in circumstances is the best guarantee for the stability of contractual relationships.

A comparative study and evaluation of the experiences of other countries can contribute towards the formulation of sound guidelines for governments engaged in selecting policy options. Abu Dhabi's experience is an appropriate case for such a comprehensive study, from which certain useful lessons can be drawn. Clearly, the participation arrangements as they have been effectively implemented in Abu Dhabi constitute the most positive aspect of Abu Dhabi's experience. These arrangements provide a radical improvement on the old-style concession system (characterized by the absolute non-involvement of the host country). They also provide a satisfactory, acceptable alternative – from a political, economic and psychological standpoint – to the 100 percent takeover of concessions.

However, developing countries which are still in the early stages of their petroleum activities should adopt a realistic attitude when studying the experiences of older producers. They should resist the temptation to emulate the practices of countries with well-established petroleum industries and proven resources, and to adopt their latest agreements containing the most favorable terms and conditions. Instead, such producers should consider the practices of countries with similar petroleum potential and geological and geographical conditions.

By the same token, oil companies should refrain from taking advantage of their superior bargaining position in the early stages of production, due to the lack of knowledge in the country concerned about its petroleum potential, and its need for foreign expertise and capabilities. It would be shortsighted to secure from such a country one-sided, onerous and rigid terms and conditions which are intended to be applicable throughout the long duration of an agreement regardless of any possible future changes in the relevant circumstances. Undoubtedly, the existence of such conditions imposed by the oil companies is bound to breed discontent and inequity in the country concerned at a later date—perhaps when oil has been discovered in commercial quantities and/or the relative bargaining position shifts in favor of the host country.

In order to ensure the smooth implementation of oil agreements, the continuation of relationships based on good faith, the mutual satisfaction of the parties involved throughout the long duration of the agreement, and to avoid situations where a host country may feel compelled to take unilateral action to redress a situation felt to be inequitable and disadvantageous, it is imperative that the legal framework covering petroleum agreements should be made equitable from the start by recognizing the legitimate interests of both parties. Since "prevention is better than cure," the parties should also anticipate the possible need for future changes and stipulate suitable provisions to allow such changes to be made in an orderly fashion in order to maintain a reasonable balance between the legitimate long-term interests of both parties.

APPENDICES

Appendix I

Text of Law No. 4 of 1976
Promulgating the Emirate of Abu Dhabi's Ownership of Gas

We, Zayed Bin Sultan Al Nahyan, Ruler of Abu Dhabi, further to

- Law No. (1) of 1974 concerning the re-organization of the government system in the Emirate of Abu Dhabi and amendments thereto;
- Law No. (2) of 1971 concerning the National Consultative Assembly;
- Law No. (7) of 1971 concerning the establishment of Abu Dhabi National Oil Company; and
- submission of the Chairman of the Board of Directors of Abu Dhabi National Oil Company and the President of the Petroleum Department, and approval of the Executive Council of the Emirate of Abu Dhabi and the National Consultative Assembly,

hereby promulgate the following law:

Article 1

All gas which is already discovered or will be discovered in the territory of the Emirate of Abu Dhabi and which is recovered or produced from oil and gas wells in the Emirate, shall be solely owned by the Emirate of Abu Dhabi. The territory of the Emirate of Abu Dhabi shall include its land, territorial water and continental shelf.

Article 2

In the application of the provision of the proceeding Article, the word "gas" shall mean:

1. Associated gas.
2. Gas caps of oil reservoirs.
3. Natural gas not associated with oil.

4. All contents of above-mentioned gases, which include:

    (a) Methane, ethane, propane and butane;

    (b) Natural gasoline and condensates from pentane to pentane 4.

Article 3

The Emirate of Abu Dhabi shall solely have the right to dispose of all quantities of gas referred to in the preceding Article, and the Emirate shall exercise its rights of ownership of such gas as follows:

1. For gas associated with oil, at the points where gas leaves the gas/oil separators throughout all stages of the separation process.

2. For gas contained in gas caps, and for natural gas not associated with oil, at wellheads.

Article 4

Abu Dhabi National Oil Company shall have the right to exploit and use all quantities of gas referred to in Article 1 of this Law as well as the right to handle all other matters related to such gas. All rights acquired through oil agreements concluded by the Government of the Emirate of Abu Dhabi in connection with discovered or produced gas or with the facilities for the recovery and production of gas, shall devolve to Abu Dhabi National Oil Company.

Article 5

All oil companies operating in the Emirate of Abu Dhabi shall deliver all gas produced from oil and gas fields to Abu Dhabi National Oil company in accordance with such conditions and technical arrangements as may be laid down by Abu Dhabi National Oil company after consultation with such companies.

Article 6

Abu Dhabi National Oil Company shall have the right to exploit the gas referred to in Article 1 of this Law either on its own or through agreements or joint ventures concluded with other parties. In the latter case, the share of Abu Dhabi National Oil Company shall not be less than 51 percent of the capital.

Article 7

Abu Dhabi National Oil Company shall make available to the oil companies operating in the Emirate of Abu Dhabi, free of charge, all quantities of gas required for their operations connected with oil production from fields covered by Agreements between the Government and such companies, as well as the quantities of gas required for lifting oil from wells by the use of gas, maintaining reservoir pressure and applying secondary recovery methods.

Article 8

Any provision inconsistent with the provisions of this Law, shall be revoked.

Article 9

This Law shall be published in the Official Gazette, and shall be put into effect as of the date of publication.

(Sgd.) ZAYED BIN SULTAN AL NAHYAN
Ruler of Abu Dhabi

(Sgd.) HAMDAN BIN MUHAMMAD AL NAHYAN
Vice-President of the Executive Council

Issued in Abu Dhabi on 1st Rabi' Al-Awal 1396 H.
Corresponding to 1st March 1976.

Appendix II

Text of Law No. 1 of 1988
Concerning the Establishment of the Supreme Petroleum Council

We, Zayed Bin Sultan Al Nahyan, Ruler of Abu Dhabi, after perusal of

- Law No. (1) of 1974 concerning the re-organization of government system in the Emirate of Abu Dhabi and amendments thereto;
- Law No. (2) of 1971 concerning the National Consultative Council and amendments thereto;
- and Law No. (7) of 1971 concerning the establishment of Abu Dhabi National Oil Company and amendments thereto;
- and Pursuant to the approval of the Executive Council, have issued the following law:

Article 1

A Council for managing petroleum affairs in the Emirate of Abu Dhabi shall be established under the name "Supreme Petroleum Council" which shall have a corporate personality and shall enjoy a financial and administrative independence in all its affairs. The Council is entitled to take all actions necessary for managing its activities in order to achieve its objectives.

Article 2

The Supreme Petroleum Council shall be the highest machinery in charge of the petroleum affairs in the Emirate, shall lay down the Emirate's petroleum policy and its objectives in all sectors of the petroleum industry and shall issue resolutions for implementing its policy and follow up such resolutions until the achievement of the aspired results. To fully attend to its duties, the Council shall lay down the necessary rules and bases in the petroleum field to govern the Emirate's dealings with all affiliates and other companies.

The Council shall issue the resolutions, follow up their implementation, verify and approve their budget. The Council shall issue necessary resolutions for managing the companies owned by the Government of Abu Dhabi. The Council will take over all the responsibilities of the Petroleum Department as well as those of the board of directors of Abu Dhabi National Oil Company.

Article 3

The Council shall have its headquarters in the city of Abu Dhabi, and may hold its meetings in any other place in the Emirate of Abu Dhabi.

Article 4

All departments, bodies, corporations and companies that are operating in the petroleum sector in the Emirate of Abu Dhabi shall comply with and carry out all decisions of the Council in order to ensure the achievement of the objectives behind its creation.

Article 5

The Chairman, Members and Secretary General of the Council shall be appointed by an Emiri Decree upon a proposal by the Chairman of the Executive Council.

Article 6

The Supreme Petroleum Council shall issue the necessary financial, administrative, internal and executive regulations by a resolution made by it.

Article 7

Article Ten of the said Law No. (7) of 1971, as amended, shall be canceled, so shall be canceled Clause No. (7) of Law No. (5) of 1987 for amending Law No. (1) of 1974 for Re-organization of the Government System in the Emirate of Abu Dhabi concerning the establishment of the Petroleum Department, and the Executive Council shall distribute the needed employees in other departments. Any text contrary to the provisions of this Law shall be canceled.

Article 8

This Law shall be implemented, shall come into force commencing its issue date, and shall be published in the Gazette.

Zayed Bin Sultan Al Nahyan
Ruler of Abu Dhabi

Khalifa Bin Zayed Al Nahyan
Chairman of Executive Council

Issued by us in Abu Dhabi
21 Shawal 1408 H.
Corresponding to June 5, 1988.

Appendix III

*The ADNOC Group of Companies**

Exploration and Production of Oil and Gas

Abu Dhabi Company for Onshore Oil Operations (ADCO); ADNOC share: 60%.

Abu Dhabi Marine Operating Company (ADMA-OPCO); ADNOC share: 60%.

Zakum Development Company (ZADCO); ADNOC share: 60%.

Oil and Gas Processing

Abu Dhabi Gas Industries Limited (GASCO); ADNOC share: 68%.

Abu Dhabi Gas Liquefaction Company Limited (ADGAS): ADNOC share: 70%.

Abu Dhabi Oil Refining Company (TAKREER); ADNOC share: 100%.

Exploration and Production Services

National Drilling Company (NDC); ADNOC share: 100%.

National Petroleum Construction Company (NPCC); ADNOC share: 70%.

Esnaad; ADNOC share: 100%.

Abu Dhabi Petroleum Ports Operating Company (IRSHAD); ADNOC share: 100%.

Chemicals and Petrochemicals

Ruwais Fertilizer Industries (FERTIL); ADNOC share: 66.66%.

Abu Dhabi Polymers Company Limited (Borouge); ADNOC share: 60%.

Maritime Transportation

Abu Dhabi National Tanker Company (ADNATCO); ADNOC share: 100%.

National Gas Shipping Company (NGSCO); ADNOC share: 70%.

Refined Products Distribution

ADNOC Distribution; ADNOC share: 100%.

---

* Source: ADNOC publication, Abu Dhabi National Oil Company and its Group of Companies, 2005.

Appendix IV

Excerpt from the Deminex Agreement of 1981

"Article 17: Taxation

The Company shall, with respect to its net income from operations under this agreement, pay basic income tax at 55 percent. If the production of Crude Oil during a calendar year shall reach an average of 100,000 (one hundred thousand) barrels per day, the Company shall pay income tax at 65 percent. If the production of Crude Oil during a calendar year shall reach an average of 200,000 (two hundred thousand) barrels per day, the Company shall pay income tax at 85 percent.

Assessment and payment of income tax shall be subject to the following provisions:

(A) The Abu Dhabi Income Tax Decree shall be supplemented as follows:

(1-a) The Company shall determine its income from operations under this Agreement and shall declare and pay the Government its income tax in respect thereof.

(1-b) If a separate non-profit making company is formed to carry out any operations under this Agreement, it is hereby agreed that such company shall be deemed to have neither income nor expenses but the Company shall include in its determination under sub-paragraph (a) above such company's actual income and expenses arising from its operations.

(1-c) In the case referred to under (b) above, the total income tax due to the Government from the Company as aforesaid for any income tax year shall not be less than the income tax which would have been due if the company had carried out itself all operations under this Agreement.

(1-d) In determining the liability to income tax of the Company in respect of its net income from operations under this Agreement no account shall be taken of any income which that Company may derive from costs or expenses which it may incur in respect of any other operations in Abu Dhabi whether under a concession agreement or otherwise and the Company shall maintain its financial records accordingly. Provided that where costs or expenses are incurred which are common to operations under this Agreement and other operations, such costs and expenses shall be apportioned between operations in accordance with sound accounting principles.

(2-a) Taxable income shall be the aggregate value of Petroleum exported or sold by the Company or delivered to the Government as royalty in kind after deducting costs and expenses fairly, properly and necessarily attributable to the operation of the Company in Abu Dhabi computed in accordance with the provisions of the Abu Dhabi Income Tax Decree. But for the purpose of calculating the annual allowances referred to in paragraph (1) (c) of Article (6) of the said Decree the reasonable percentage in respect of intangible assets shall be 5 percent per annum and in respect of physical assets shall be 10 percent per annum and this provision shall be deemed to be an agreement of the kind referred to in paragraph (2) (b) of the said Article (6).

(2-b) The aggregate value of any petroleum delivered to the Government as royalty in kind shall be the aggregate of the amounts credited for the purpose of royalty in accordance with Article 13(A) thereof.

(2-c) In the event that the company disposes of any technical information or know-how which has been gained by or used in operations under this agreement the amount or value of any consideration received by the Company for the disposal shall, so far as it is not taken into account in computing the costs and expenses deducted in determining the taxable income of the company as aforesaid, be treated for all purposes as part of the Company taxable income.

(3)   In the case of Crude Oil exported by the Company from Abu Dhabi, the aggregate value referred to in paragraph (2) above shall not be less than the amount which results from multiplying the number of barrels of such Crude Oil exported by the applicable Posted Price per barrel.

(4)   In the determination of taxable income, nothing in this Agreement shall be construed as permitting the deduction, either as an expense of the year or by way of depreciation or amortization, of the following items:

(a) Foreign taxation paid on income derived from sources within Abu Dhabi.

(b) Interest or other consideration paid or suffered by the Company in respect of the financing of its operations in Abu Dhabi.

(c) Expenditure in relation to the organizing and initiating of Petroleum operations in Abu Dhabi.

(d) Bonuses paid to the Government under Article 10 of this Agreement.

(e) Rentals to the Government under Article 2 of this Agreement.

(B) Within thirty (30) days of the end of each quarter of the income tax year the Company shall submit to the Government a provisional tonnage statement showing the quantity of Crude Oil exported by it during the period from the preceding 1st day of January to the end of that quarter and such other information as may reasonably be required to enable the Government to calculate the amount of the payments due by the Company hereunder and the Company shall estimate and pay the amount of income tax due from it to the Government in respect of that quarter. Such estimate shall be based on the latest information of costs, expenses, quantities and prices and shall be cumulative for the income tax year in question so that in estimating the amount payable in respect of each quarter there shall be deducted the total amount of any payments for previous quarter of the Income tax year. On or before the 15th day of the fourth month following the end of each income tax year the company shall submit to the Government a final tonnage statement and shall file its income tax declaration for such year at the office of the Director of Income Tax. If as a result of such declaration any amount shall be due to the Government, the Company shall pay the balance forthwith. If as a result of such declaration any amount shall have been found to have been overpaid to the Government by the Company, it shall be carried forward and treated as a payment on account for the current income tax year.

(C) The Government has the right to appoint auditors to examine the books and records of the Company on its behalf."

"Article 18: Limit of Taxation

Except for payments provided for in Article 17 hereof, no other or higher taxes, impositions, duties, fees or charges shall be imposed upon the Company or upon its property, privileges or employees or upon the latter's property, privileges or employees within Abu Dhabi, other than those ordinarily imposed and generally applicable to other companies engaged in similar operations in Abu Dhabi. No tax, impositions, duty, fee, charge or levy shall be imposed upon the borings, products, materials, equipment, installations or plants of the company in Abu Dhabi, or upon any of the substances comprised in Article 21 hereof and used by the Company for the purpose of its operations authorized by this Agreement, or upon any distribution by the Company of its income from or investment in operations authorized by this Agreement."

[183]

NOTES

Introduction

1. *Arab Oil and Gas Directory*, 2005 (Paris: Arab Petroleum Research Center), 490.

2. *Arab Oil and Gas Directory*, 2006 (Paris: Arab Petroleum Research Center), 514.

3. Ibid.

4. The Constitution of the United Arab Emirates promulgated on December 2, 1971, Article 23.

5. The UAE Civil Transactions Code (Federal Law No. 5 of 1985), Article 1206.

Chapter 1

1. Charles Issawi and Mohammed Yeganeh, *The Economics of Middle Eastern Oil* (New York, NY: Frederick A. Praeger, 1962), 24.

2. Ibid., 24–39; and Mana Al Otaiba, *Petroleum and the Economy of the United Arab Emirates* (London: Croom Helm, 1977), 38.

3. Issawi and Yeganeh, op. cit., 23–24.

4. Ibid., 23.

5. Fadhil Al Chalabi, *OPEC and the International Oil Industry: A Changing Structure*, published by Oxford University Press on behalf of the Organization of Arab Petroleum Exporting Countries (OAPEC), 1980, 16.

6. Al Otaiba, op. cit., 106.

7. Al Chalabi, op. cit., 17.

8. Ibid., 16.

9. Ibid., 23–24.

10. *Arab Oil and Gas Directory*, 2005, op. cit., 361, 366.

11. Ibid., 20

12. Issawi and Yaganeh, op. cit., 9.

13. Ibid., 10–11.

14. Benjamin Shwadran, *The Middle East, Oil and The Great Powers* (New York, NY: Council for Middle Eastern Affairs Press, 1959), 440, 442.

15. Stephen Longrigg, *Oil in the Middle East: Its Discovery and Development* (London/Toronto/New York, NY: Oxford University Press, 3rd ed., 1968), 475.

16. Most of the factual material for this historical introduction is derived from: Paul Stevens, *Joint Ventures in Middle East Oil 1957–1976* (Beirut: Middle East Economic Consultants (MEEC), 1976); and Muhamad Mughrabi, *Permanent Sovereignty over Oil Resources* (Beirut: Middle East Economic Research and Publishing Center, 1966).

17. Mughrabi, op. cit., 14.

18. See, Stevens, op. cit., 131. On the general subject of permanent sovereignty see Kamal Hossain and Subrata Chowdhury, *Permanent Sovereignty over Natural Resources in International Law: Principle and Practice* (London, Frances Pinter Publishers, 1984).

19. Mughrabi, op. cit., 62–64; and Paul Frankel, *Mattei: Oil and Power Politics* (London: Faber and Faber, 1966).

20. The Information presented in this section is taken from two main sources: Mana Al Otaiba, *Petroleum and the Economy of the United Arab Emirates* (London: Croom Helm, 1977), 45–64; and *The Oil Industry in Abu Dhabi and Qatar* (Beirut: Middle East Economic Consultants (MEEC), report no. 31, January 1979).

21. MEEC, op. cit., 40.

22. Al Otaiba, op. cit., 76.

23. The Economist Intelligence Unit, *Country Report: The UAE*, October 2002; *The Middle East and North Africa* (London/New York, NY: Europe Publications, 2004), 1179–1180; and *Arab Oil and Gas Directory*, 2005, op. cit., 487.

24. *Arab Oil and Gas Directory*, 2005, op. cit., 480.

25. The Economist Intelligence Unit, op. cit.; *The Middle East and North Africa*, op. cit., 1179; and *Arab Oil and Gas Directory*, 2005, op. cit., 487.

26. Al Otaiba, op. cit., 85.

27. The Economist Intelligence Unit, op. cit.; *The Middle East and North Africa*, op. cit., 1180; and *Arab Oil and Gas Directory*, 2005, op. cit., 487.

28. *The Middle East and North Africa*, op. cit., 1180.

29. *Arab Oil and Gas Directory*, 2006, op. cit., 524.

30. MEEC, op. cit., 38.

31. *Arab Oil and Gas Directory*, 2005, op. cit., 487.

32. *Arab Oil and Gas Directory*, 2006, op. cit.,514.

33. MEEC, op. cit., 43, quoting an estimate made by the UAE Minister of Petroleum and Mineral Resources in early 1977.

34. *ADNOC's Five Year Achievements Report: 2000–2004* (http://www.adnoc.com/adnoc/English/ADNOC_English_final_Hi%Res.pdf).

Chapter 2

1. *Expensing of royalty*: In the initial profit-sharing agreement with Saudi Arabia in 1950 and similar agreements with other producing countries of the region (Kuwait, Iraq, etc.) the equal profit sharing concept was

implemented on the understanding that the total of the royalty and the income tax paid by the concessionaire would be equal to 50% of net profits and would represent the producing country's overall share. Consequently, royalty payments were not deducted from income as an expense item in computing the income tax, but were instead credited against the tax payable to the producing country. OPEC was successful (in the period 1964–1965) in obtaining the agreement of most of the oil companies operating in the producing countries concerned on what is described in the oil industry's language as the "expensing" of royalties. The principle underlying the agreement is henceforth to treat royalty payments as an expense in computing income tax instead of a credit against the income tax.

2. Al Otaiba, op. cit, 41.

3. Ibid.

4. *Phase-in* and *bridging* oil: According to the general Agreement on Participation of 1972, the twenty-five percent ownership interest entitled the host country to an equal proportion of the crude oil produced by the company operating therein, but it was agreed that part of this entitlement be sold back to the concerned companies as "bridging oil"—the oil from the government's twenty-five percent share which the companies needed to fulfill their existing commitments over a period of three years from the signing of the agreement. It was also stipulated that the companies would – if required by the government concerned – purchase additional quantities of the government share to assist the latter enter the market gradually. This kind of oil was referred to as "phase-in" oil. See: Al Otaiba, op. cit., 260–261; and MEEC, op. cit., 19–20.

5. The consortium headed by Mitsubishi that concluded a concession agreement on 14 May, 1968 with Abu Dhabi was composed of the following companies: Mitsubish Mining Co. Ltd.; Mitsubish Shoji Kaisha Ltd.; Mitsubish heavy Industries Ltd.; Mitsubish Oil Co. Ltd.; and Mitsubish Petrochemical Co. Ltd.

6. See: Claude Duval, K. Blinn, H. Le Leuch and A. Pertuzio, *International Petroleum Exploration and Exploitation Agreements* (New York, NY: Barrows, 1986); and J. Kinna, "Recent Trends in Petroleum Regions," paper submitted to the International Bar Association (IBA) Seminar on Energy Law in Asia and the Pacific, Singapore 1982.

7. For the full text of this agreement, concluded on May 3, 1981, see: Mana Al Otaiba, *The Petroleum Concession Agreements of the United Arab Emirates, 1972–1981* (London: Croom Helm, 1982).

8. Law No. 4 of 1976 on the emirate of Abu Dhabi's ownership of gas, promulgated on March 1, 1976. See full text in Appendix I.

9. See the Deminex agreement, available in Mana Al Otaiba, *The Petroleum Concession Agreements of the United Arab Emirates*, op. cit.

10. *Under expenditure*: This is the exact wording of this provision in the Deminex Agreement. It means the amounts of money which should have been spent by the concessionaire under Article 6 of the agreement (work obligations), but were not effectively spent.

11. Deminex Agreement, available in Mana Al Otaiba, *The Petroleum Concession Agreements of the United Arab Emirates*, op. cit., Article 12.

12. Ibid., Article 14.

13. Ibid., Article 35.

14. In this context, one may cite the comments of Professor Ahmed Kosheri, Professor of International Law at the University of Cairo and a well-known international arbitrator: "However, the promulgation of a special law granting to the concession agreement the binding legal force ... does not transform the nature of the contractual provisions or convert them into statutory rules ..." He also refers to the "[I]mportance of keeping in mind that the provisions of a petroleum agreement remain contractual in nature even after being given the force of law ..." Kosheri concludes: "To the best of our knowledge there is no single case or authority supporting the idea that a contractual provision provided with the force of

[189]

law has to be treated as a statutory rule …" Ahmad Kosheri, "The Particularity of the Conflict Avoidance Methods Pertaining to Petroleum Agreements," paper submitted to the International Conference on the Settlement of Energy and Oil and Gas Disputes, held in Cairo, Egypt, November 18–19, 1995, 19, 20, 22.

15. Blinn, Duval, Le Leuch and Pertuzio, op. cit., 308–309.

16. Deminex Agreement, available in Mana Al Otaiba, *The Petroleum Concession Agreements of the United Arab Emirates*, op. cit., Article 38.

17. Ibid., Article 44.

18. According to Article 45, these hydrocarbon processing activities include; production and export of methane, nitrogen fertilizer; and the recovery and export of LPG or LNG. It should be noted that these processing activities do not come under the standard obligations of a concessionaire in an exploration and production concession (the normal obligations only include exploration for petroleum and then, if commercial discovery is achieved, development and production of the petroleum discovered). This article of the agreement obliges the concessionaire to study the feasibility of these extra activities and execute them, if feasible, when its operations prove to be profitable (the criteria of profitability here is to achieve a production of not less than 100,000 bpd). The execution of these activities will then be considered as a contribution from the concessionaire to the economic development of the national economy of the host country. It is interesting in this context to remark that paragraph (D) of this article states: "The company undertakes to invest at least ten (10%) percent of its profits in one or more of the above mentioned projects whose economic viability has been established."

19. *Law No. 4 of 1976*, op. cit.

Chapter 3

1. The law establishing ADNOC (Law No.7 of 27 November 1971), Article 3. The full text of this law appears in: Mana Al Otaiba, *The Petroleum Concession Agreements of the United Arab Emirates*, op. cit.

2. It is noteworthy that this law closely followed a model established by OPEC for adoption in member countries. It provides rules and regulations according to which all operations (exploration, drilling, production, etc.) should be carried out in compliance with the most efficient scientific techniques and methods. It spells out, inter alia, precautions that should be taken to safeguard the health and safety of employees and prevent pollution, as well as the reporting obligations of operating companies to the governmental authority and the prior authorizations and permissions they have to obtain. Utilization of gas is regulated by law, which imposes fines for violations of its provisions.

3. The law establishing ADNOC (Law No. 7 of 27 November 1971), Article 19, in Al Otaiba, *The Petroleum Concession Agreements of the United Arab Emirates*, op. cit.

4. The participation agreement was concluded between Abu Dhabi and Abu Dhabi Marine Areas (ADMA) Ltd. on September 13, 1974. This excerpt comes from Article 4(i). The full text of this agreement appears in: Al Otaiba, *The Petroleum Concession Agreements of the United Arab Emirates*, op. cit.

5. "Arabization policy" is the term used in both Article 3.02 of the Implementing Agreement and Article IV(c) of the Articles of Association of ADMA-OPCO. Article 3.02 states: "In implementing its policy of hiring personnel, ADMA-OPCO shall abide by the government's policy of Arabization by recruiting by preference, nationals of the UAE, followed by other Arabs, as this policy is set forth in the recruiting rules and regulations in force in Abu Dhabi and the UAE from time to time."

6. In this context it is noteworthy that levels of production and allowables are determined by the unilateral decision of the government, as are the crude oil prices in accordance with the OPEC resolutions.

7. *OPEC Annual Statistical Bulletin*, 2005; *Arab Oil & Gas Directory*, 2006, op. cit., 514.

8. In addition, there are four other smaller operating companies contributing a small percentage of Abu Dhabi's output.

9. *Abu Dhabi National Oil Company and its Group of Companies* (Abu Dhabi: ADNOC, 2005).

10. Ibid.

11. *Arab Oil and Gas Directory*, 2005, op. cit., 487 et seq.

12. *Abu Dhabi National Oil Company and its Group of Companies*, op. cit.

13. Ibid.

14. Law establishing ADNOC, Article 3, paragraph 1, op. cit.

15. See Chapter 4 on Abu Dhabi's Gas Experience.

16. *Abu Dhabi National Oil Company and its Group of Companies*, op. cit.

17. In 2002, ADNOC established a wholly owned subsidiary called Esnaad after the merger of National Marine Services (NMS) and the Abu Dhabi Drilling Chemicals and Projects Limited (ADDCAP).

18. *Abu Dhabi National Oil Company and its Group of Companies*, op. cit.

Chapter 4

1. "Dry gas" is gas from which entrained liquids and non-hydrocarbon gases have been removed.

2. A revised estimate is yet to be released.

3. *Arab Oil and Gas Directory*, 2006 (Paris: Arab Petroleum Research Center), 509.

4. According to the Qatari Minister of Energy and Industry, gas from Qatar will begin to flow in 2007. See "H.E. Al-Attiyah Welcomes 'Opportunity to Discuss Gas Challenges' as 22nd Gastech Opens in Abu Dhabi," December 4, 2006, Qatar Petroleum website (http:// www.qp.com.qa).

5. The main source of information on the Dolphin Project is the *Arab Oil and Gas Directory*, 2005 (Paris: Arab Petroleum Research Center), specifically the section on the emirate of Abu Dhabi, 487–513. Also see the website of Dolphin Energy Ltd. (www.dolphinenergy.com).

6. Dolphin Energy Ltd. website (www.dolphinenergy.com).

7. Until 1997, ADGAS was owned by Abu Dhabi National Oil Company (51%); BP (16.33%), Compagnies Franchises des Pétroles "Total" (8.17%) and Mitsui group (24.5%). In December 1997, it was agreed between ADNOC and the other shareholders of ADGAS to increase ADNOC's shareholding to 70 percent, resulting in the present shareholding of ADGAS: ADNOC (70%), Mitsui (15%), BP (10%) and Total (5%).

8. Free on Board (FOB) denotes an arrangement whereby the seller's obligations are fulfilled when the goods are placed on board the vessel, or deposited in a location specified by the buyer.

9. A source of supply assurance may be in the form of representation (formal declarations of the parties) that an agreement relating to adequate feedstock has been reached or a recital (introduction of the agreement, preamble) that adequate feedstock will be available. Such assurances are not a significant problem for a typical seller as the gas feedstock reserve is the aim of the LNG project. Similarly, events of force majeure can be negotiated to an acceptable level of risk for both parties, as the driving force behind any LNG project is the need for continued uninterrupted sales.

10. The Incoterms are the International Chamber of Commerce (ICC) standardized trade terms. They are a universally recognized set of definitions of international trade terms. Thus, the ICC definitions of terms like FOB, CIF and C&F are an intrinsic part of commercial language. These standard abbreviations place specific obligations on buyer and seller when included in a contract. See: "Incoterms 1990," publication no. 460 of the International Chamber of Commerce (ICC), Paris, 1990; and Jan Ramberg, "Guide to Incoterms 1990," ICC publication no. 461/90, Paris, 1990.

11. "Arm's length price" refers to the price charged, in an open market, in the usual and ordinary course of lawful trade and competition, at the time of the conclusion of the contract for such goods sold under comparable circumstances in the trade concerned.

Chapter 5

1. Abu Dhabi Income Tax (Amendment) Decree of June 1, 1970.

2. Abu Dhabi Income Tax Decree No. 10 of August 5, 1970.

3. James Griffin and David J. Teece (eds), *OPEC Behavior and World Oil Prices* (London: George Allen & Unwin, 1982), 9.

4. A meeting of Petroleum Ministers in the Gulf area held in Abu Dhabi on November 9–10, 1974 preceded this decision. In this meeting a decision was made to raise the income tax rate applicable to the oil companies to 85 percent and to raise the rate of the royalty to 20 percent, while reducing the posted price of crude oil by 40 cents per barrel. The OPEC full conference (its forty-second meeting) held in Vienna on December 13, 1974 endorsed the decision made in the Abu Dhabi meeting.

5. Letter (No. AD-1/18/1507) dated November 14, 1974 from the Chairman of the Abu Dhabi Department of Petroleum addressed to ADPC and ADMA.

6. ADMA was notified of this increase by Letter No. SPC/3-1/1450, dated February 6, 1989. A similar letter was sent to ADPC.

7. The law establishing ADNOC (Law No. 7 of 1971), full text in: Al Otaiba, *Petroleum Concession Agreements of the United Arab Emirates 1939–1981*, op. cit.

8. Letter (No. M-1-3-533) dated February 19, 1979 from the Chairman of the Department of Petroleum to ADMA Ltd.

9. This section refers to oil prices. For a discussion of gas prices see Chapter 4. The information related to the historical development of prices, as outlined in this sub-section, was sourced from two main references: Abdul Amir Kubbah, *OPEC: Past and Present* (Vienna: Petro Economic Research Center, 1974); and Mana Al Otaiba, *OPEC and the Petroleum Industry* (London: Croom Helm, 1975).

Chapter 6

1. F. Rouhani, *International Agreements and Contracts in the Field of Petroleum*, 1962, 35–36.

2. Ibrahim Shihata, "The Settlement of Disputes under Oil and Gas Agreements: The Relevance of ICSID and the World Bank Group Guidelines," paper submitted to the Conference on the Settlement of Energy and International Electric Network Disputes, Cairo, November 18–19, 1995, 2–3.

3. Ibid., 3.

4. Ibid.

5. Henry Cattan, *The Law of Oil Concessions in the Middle East and North Africa* (New York, NY: Oceana Publications Inc., 1967), 143

6. Ibid., 3.

7. Ibid

8. The ADPC Concession Agreement of 1939, full text in Al Otaiba, *Petroleum Concession Agreements of the United Arab Emirates*, op. cit.

9. Shihata, op. cit.

10. Cattan, op. cit, 147.

11. This summary is based on two main sources: "Digest of Oil related Arbitral Awards," circulated by the Cairo Regional Commercial Arbitration Center during the International Conference on the Settlement of Energy, Petroleum and Gas Disputes, Cairo, Egypt, November 18–19, 1995; and Ahmed Kosheri, "Petroleum Arbitral Awards," a paper submitted to the conference on Managing Risks in International Oil and Gas Contracts, at the Cairo Regional Commercial Arbitration Center, Cairo, May 22–23, 2006.

12. Ibid.

13. Hersch Lauterpacht (ed.), *International Law Reports* (ILR), vol. 18, January 1957, 145.

14. Ibid.

15. Ibid.

16. Ibid.

17. Ibid., 161.

18. On Aramco arbitration see Kattan, op. cit., 152–153; and Kosheri, "Petroleum Arbitral Awards," op. cit., 8–13.

20. Cairo Regional Commercial Arbitration Center, "Digest of Oil related Arbitral Awards," op. cit.

21. Ibid.

22. Ibid.

23. Ibid. Full text of the award available in ILR, vol. 27, 117.

24. Kosheri, op. cit., 35–43.

25. Ibid.

26. Ibid.

27. Ibid.

28. Ibid.

29. Ibid.

30. *International Legal Materials* (ILM), vol. 21, 1982, 876.

31. For further details on the LIAMCO arbitration see: Kosheri, op. cit., 26–30.

32. Ibid.

33. Full text of award available in Albert Jan van den Berg (ed.), *Yearbook: Commercial Arbitration* vol. VI (Netherlands: Kluwer Law International, 1976), 89.

34. Quoted in Richard Bentham, "Arbitration and the Petroleum Industry," paper presented at the International Bar Association (IBA) Twentieth Biennial Conference held in Vienna, September 2–7, 1984, 1–2.

35. Ibid., 3.

36. Deminex agreement, available in Mana Al Otaiba, *The Petroleum Concession Agreements of the United Arab Emirates 1939–1981*, op. cit., Article 35.

37. From the Author's file—at the time General Counsel of ADNOC and member of the legal committee which drafted the clause. The committee also included legal advisors of some of the major companies operating in Abu Dhabi: BP, Shell, Total, etc.

Chapter 7

1. Alfred Boulos, "The Past and Present Contractual Make-up: Options for Negotiating Future Concessions," paper submitted to a conference organized by the Emirates Center for Strategic Studies and Research (ECSSR) in Abu Dhabi, October 1996, entitled: Strategic Positioning in the Oil Industry: Trends and Options.

2. Marc Lalonde, "Energy Companies and their Host Governments: To Each his Own," paper presented at the International Bar Association (IBA) Energy Law Seminar held in the Netherlands, April 1990, *Seminar Proceedings*, 41, 42, 47.

3. Ibid.

4. Atef Suleiman, "The Oil experience of the UAE and its Legal Framework," *Journal of Energy and Natural Resources Law*, vol. 6, no. 1, 1988, 24.

5. See the concession agreement of Maruzen Oil Company Ltd., December 6, 1967, Article 8. The text of this agreement appears in Mana Al Otaiba, *The Petroleum Concession Agreements of the United Arab Emirates 1939–1981*, op. cit.

6. See the concession agreement of Pan Ocean Oil Corporation, June 7, 1970, Article 8(d). The text of this agreement appears in Mana Al Otaiba, *The Petroleum Concession Agreements of the United Arab Emirates 1939–1971*, op. cit.

7. Law on the Conservation of Petroleum Resources (Law No. 8 of 1978), Article 56.

8. *Health, Safety and Environment Management System (HSEMS)*, circulated by ADNOC in 1997, 45.

9. Ibid., 23

10. Ibid.

11. Ibid.

12. The joint venture agreement between ADNOC, CFP, Shell and Partex, signed on July 23, 1978 for the establishment of Abu Dhabi Gas Industries Ltd. (GASCO).

Chapter 8

1. *Arab Oil and Gas Directory, 2005* (Paris: Arab Petroleum Research Center), 510.

2. *ADNOC: Five Year Achievement Report (2000–2004)* on ADNOC website (www.adnoc.com).

BIBLIOGRAPHY

Abu Dhabi National Oil Company and its Group of Companies 2005 (Abu Dhabi: ADNOC, 2005).

ADNOC: Five Year Achievement Report (2000–2004) (www.adnoc.com).

Al Chalabi, Fadhil. *OPEC and the International Oil Industry: A Changing Structure* (London/Toronto/New York, NY: Oxford University Press, on behalf of OAPEC, 1980).

Al Otaiba, Mana Saeed. *OPEC and the Petroleum Industry* (London: Croom Helm, 1975).

Al Otaiba, Mana Saeed. *The Petroleum Concession Agreements of the United Arab Emirates 1939–1981* (London: Croom Helm, 1982).

Al Otaiba, Mana Saeed. *Petroleum and the Economy of the United Arab Emirates* (London: Croom Helm, 1977).

Arab Petroleum Research Center. *Arab Oil and Gas Directory* (Paris: Arab Petroleum Research Center, 2005).

Barberis, Daniele. *Negotiating Mining Agreements: Past, Present and Future Trends* (London: Kluwer Law International, 1998).

Bentham, Richard. *Arbitration and the Petroleum Industry*. International Bar Association (IBA) Twentieth Biennial Conference, Vienna, 2–7 September, 1984.

Blinn, K., C. Duval, H. Le Leuch and A. Pertuzio. *International Petroleum Exploration and Exploitation Agreements* (New York, NY: Barrows, 1986).

Boulos, Alfred. *The Past and Present Contractual Make-up: Options for Negotiating Future Concessions*. Emirates Center for Strategic Studies and Research conference: "Strategic Positioning in the Oil Industry: Trends and Options," Abu Dhabi, October 1996.

Boulos, Alfred. *Mutuality of Interests between Companies and Governments – Myth or Fact.* "Energy Law Seminar," International Bar Association (IBA), Netherlands, April 1990.

Cameron, Peter. *Arbitration in the Energy Sector and Recent Developments.* "Seminar on Arbitration in Petroleum and other Energy Contracts," Abu Dhabi, 13–14 October, 1998.

Cattan, Henry. *The Evolution of Oil Concessions in the Middle East and North Africa.* Parker School of Foreign and Comparative Law (New York, NY: Oceana Publications Inc., 1967).

Gao, Zhigno. "International Petroleum Exploration and Exploitation Agreements: A Comprehensive Environmental Appraisal." *Journal of Energy and Natural Resources Law*, vol. 10, no. 4, 1992.

Griffin, James and David J. Teece (eds). *OPEC Behavior and World Oil Prices* (London: George Allen & Unwin, 1982).

Hossain K. and S. Chowdhury. *Permanent Sovereignty over Natural Resources in International Law: Principle and Practice* (London, Frances Pinter Publishers, 1984).

International Legal Materials, vol. 21, 1982.

Issawi, Charles and Yeganeh, Mohammed. *The Economics of Middle Eastern Oil* (New York, NY: Frederick A. Praeger, 1962).

Kosheri, Ahmed. "Petroleum Arbitral Awards." Paper submitted to a Conference on Managing Risks in International Oil and Gas Contracts at the Cairo Regional Commercial Arbitration Center, Cairo, May 22–23, 2006.

Kosheri, Ahmed. "The Particularity of the Conflict Avoidance Methods Pertaining to Petroleum Agreements." Paper presented at the

International Conference on the Settlement of Energy, Petroleum and Gas disputes, Cairo, November, 1995.

Kosheri, Ahmed. "Contemporary Approach in the Contracts of Exploration of Energy in the Arab World." Seminar on Arbitration in Petroleum and Other Energy Contracts, Abu Dhabi, 13–14 October, 1998.

Kinna, J.C. "Recent Trends in Petroleum Regimes." Paper submitted to the International Bar Association (IBA) Seminar on Energy Law in Asia and the Pacific, Singapore, 1982.

Kubbah, A. *OPEC, Past and Present* (Vienna: Petro-Economic Research Center, 1974).

Lalonde, Marc. "Energy Companies and their Host Governments: To Each His Own." International Bar Association (IBA) Energy Law Seminar, Netherlands, April 1990.

Lauterpacht, Hersch (ed.) *International Law Reports* (ILR), vol. 18, January 1957, 145.

Longrigg, Stephen Hemsley. *Oil in the Middle East: Its Discovery and Development* (London: Oxford University Press, 1968).

Mughrabi, M.A. *Permanent Sovereignty over Oil Resources* (Beirut: Middle East Economic Research and Publishing Center, 1966).

OAPEC Annual Statistical Report 2006 (www.oapec.org/images/A%205% 20R%202006.pdf).

OPEC Annual Statistical Bulletin 2005 (Vienna: OPEC, 2005).

Rouhani, Fuad. *International Agreements and Contracts in the Field of Petroleum* (1962).

Shihata, Ibrahim. *The Settlement of Disputes under Oil and Gas Exploration and Development Agreements: The Relevance of ICSID and the World Bank Group Guidelines.* "Conference on the Settlement of Energy and International Electric Network Disputes," Cairo, November 18–19, 1995.

Shwadran, Benjamin. *The Middle East, Oil and the Great Powers* (New York, NY: Council for Middle Eastern Affairs Press, 1959).

Suleiman, Atef. *Arbitration in Petroleum Contracts.* "Seminar on Arbitration in Petroleum and Other Energy Contracts," Abu Dhabi, October 13–14, 1998.

Suleiman, Atef. "The Oil Experience of the United Arab Emirates and its Legal Framework." *Journal of Energy and Natural Resources Law*, vol. 6, no.1, 1988.

Suleiman, Atef. "Certain Aspects of the Gas Experience of the UAE." *Journal of Energy and Natural Resources Law*, vol. 13, no. 3, 1995.

Stevens, Paul I. *Joint Ventures in Middle East Oil 1957–1975* (Beirut: Middle East Economic Consultants, 1976).

Walde, Thomas. "Investment Arbitration under the Energy Charter Treaty." Paper submitted to the Seminar on Arbitration in Petroleum and Other Energy Contracts, Abu Dhabi, October 13–14, 1998.

Walde, Thomas, "Environmental Policies towards Mining in Developing Countries." *Journal of Energy and Natural Resources Law*, vol. 10, no. 4, 1992.

Yamani, Ahmed Zaki. "Participation versus Nationalization," in Mikdashi Z. (ed.), *Continuity and Change in World Oil Industry*. (Beirut: The Middle East Economic Research and Publishing Center, 1969).

Dr. Atef Suleiman was General Counsel and Manager of the Legal Department of the Abu Dhabi National Oil Company (ADNOC) from 1974 to the end of 1997 and has been involved in legal and economic aspects of the oil industry for more than forty years through his employment in major oil producing nations of the Middle East.

Dr. Suleiman's previous positions include: Petroleum Consultant for Legal and Economic Affairs to the Algerian national oil company Sonatrach (1968–1974); Associate at Tariki Oil Consultancy Firm, Beirut (1965–1968); Legal Advisor at the Ministry of Energy and Industry, Algeria (1964–1965); and Legal Advisor, then Director of the Legal Department at the Saudi Arabian Ministry of Petroleum and Mineral Affairs (1957–1964).

Dr. Suleiman served on a UAE Special Committee appointed by the State for drafting various federal laws including the Commercial Law, Commercial Maritime Law and Commercial Companies Law.

He is a member of the Jordanian Bar Association; the International Bar Association (since 1980); the International Law Association; and the Arab Association for International Commercial Arbitration.

He has also served on a number of arbitration panels including that of the Euro-Arab Chambers of Commerce, Paris; the American Arbitration Association; the Cairo Regional Centre for International Commercial Arbitration; the GCC Commercial Arbitration Centre, Bahrain; and the Abu Dhabi Commercial Conciliation and Arbitration Center.

Dr. Suleiman has written extensively on the legal and economic aspects of the international petroleum industry and has published three books and numerous articles for specialized journals.

Dr. Suleiman received a Bachelor of Laws (LLB) from the University of Cairo; and a Doctor of Laws from the University of Paris. He is fluent in Arabic, English and French.

INDEX